KAIJUMAX
SEASON TWO
THE SEAMY UNDERBELLY

KAIJUMAX SEASON TWO

THE SEAMY UNDERBELLY

怪獣マックス

By Zander Cannon

Color assists by Jason Fischer

Designed by Dylan Todd
Logo by Zander Cannon

Edited by Charlie Chu

An Oni Press Publication

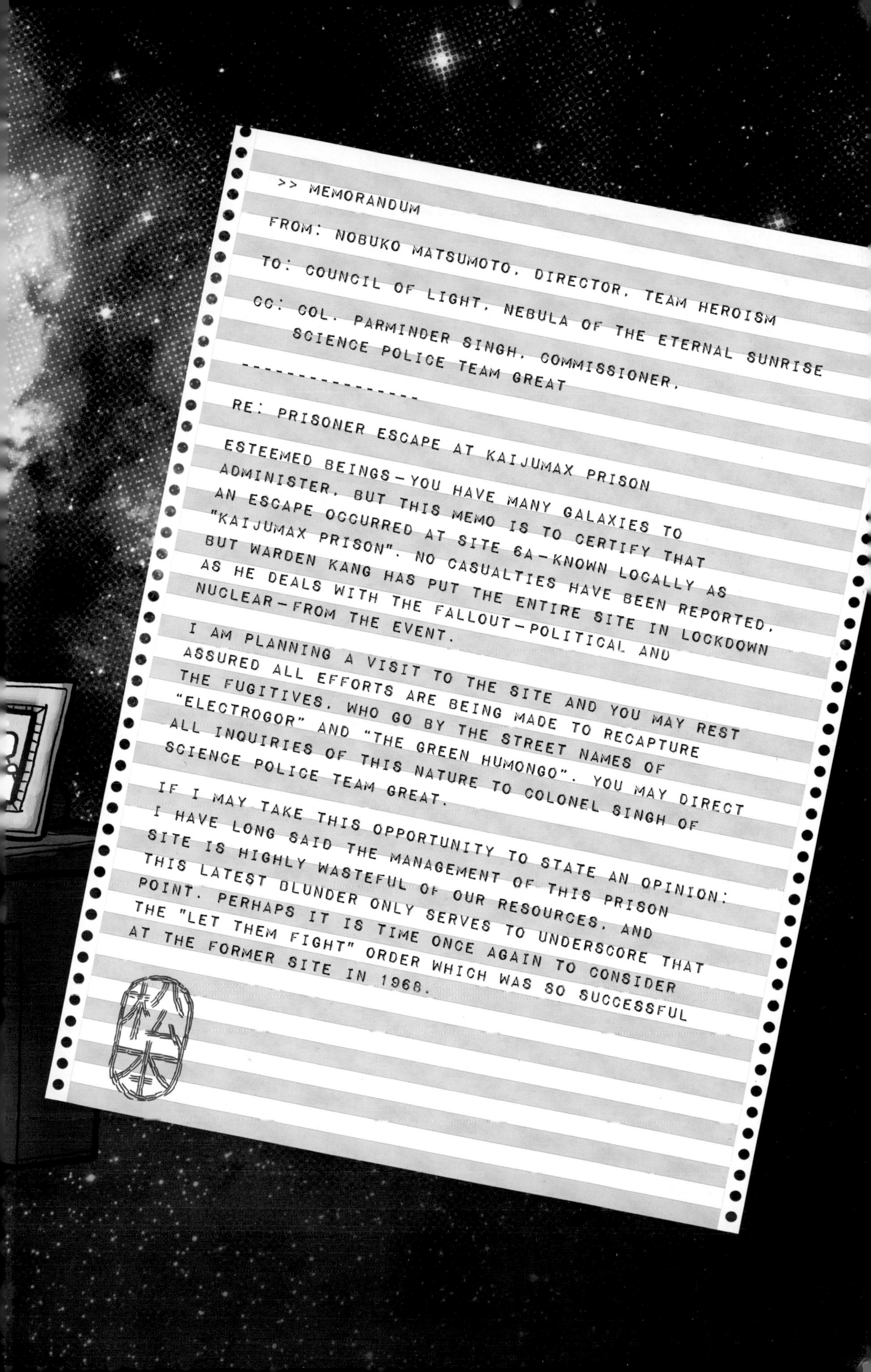

>> MEMORANDUM

FROM: NOBUKO MATSUMOTO, DIRECTOR, TEAM HEROISM

TO: COUNCIL OF LIGHT, NEBULA OF THE ETERNAL SUNRISE

CC: COL. PARMINDER SINGH, COMMISSIONER,
SCIENCE POLICE TEAM GREAT

RE: PRISONER ESCAPE AT KAIJUMAX PRISON

ESTEEMED BEINGS—YOU HAVE MANY GALAXIES TO ADMINISTER, BUT THIS MEMO IS TO CERTIFY THAT AN ESCAPE OCCURRED AT SITE 6A—KNOWN LOCALLY AS "KAIJUMAX PRISON". NO CASUALTIES HAVE BEEN REPORTED, BUT WARDEN KANG HAS PUT THE ENTIRE SITE IN LOCKDOWN AS HE DEALS WITH THE FALLOUT—POLITICAL AND NUCLEAR—FROM THE EVENT.

I AM PLANNING A VISIT TO THE SITE AND YOU MAY REST ASSURED ALL EFFORTS ARE BEING MADE TO RECAPTURE THE FUGITIVES, WHO GO BY THE STREET NAMES OF "ELECTROGOR" AND "THE GREEN HUMONGO". YOU MAY DIRECT ALL INQUIRIES OF THIS NATURE TO COLONEL SINGH OF SCIENCE POLICE TEAM GREAT.

IF I MAY TAKE THIS OPPORTUNITY TO STATE AN OPINION: I HAVE LONG SAID THE MANAGEMENT OF THIS PRISON SITE IS HIGHLY WASTEFUL OF OUR RESOURCES, AND THIS LATEST BLUNDER ONLY SERVES TO UNDERSCORE THAT POINT. PERHAPS IT IS TIME ONCE AGAIN TO CONSIDER THE "LET THEM FIGHT" ORDER WHICH WAS SO SUCCESSFUL AT THE FORMER SITE IN 1968.

Published by Oni Press, Inc.
Joe Nozemack, publisher
James Lucas Jones, editor in chief
Andrew McIntire, v.p. of marketing & sales
David Dissanayake, sales manager
Rachel Reed, publicity coordinator
Troy Look, director of design & production
Hilary Thompson, graphic designer
Angie Dobson, digital prepress technician
Ari Yarwood, managing editor
Charlie Chu, senior editor
Robin Herrera, editor
Bess Pallares, editorial assistant
Brad Rooks, director of logistics
Jung Lee, logistics associate

onipress.com
facebook.com/onipress
twitter.com/onipress
onipress.tumblr.com
instagram.com/onipress

zandercannon.com / @zander_cannon

KAIJUMAX.COM

studiojfish.com / @studiojfish

This volume collects issues #1-6 of the Oni Press series *Kaijumax: Season Two*.

First edition: April 2017

ISBN 978-1-62010-396-8
eISBN 978-1-62010-397-5

PRINTED IN CHINA.

Library of Congress Control Number: 2016955402

1 2 3 4 5 6 7 8 9 10

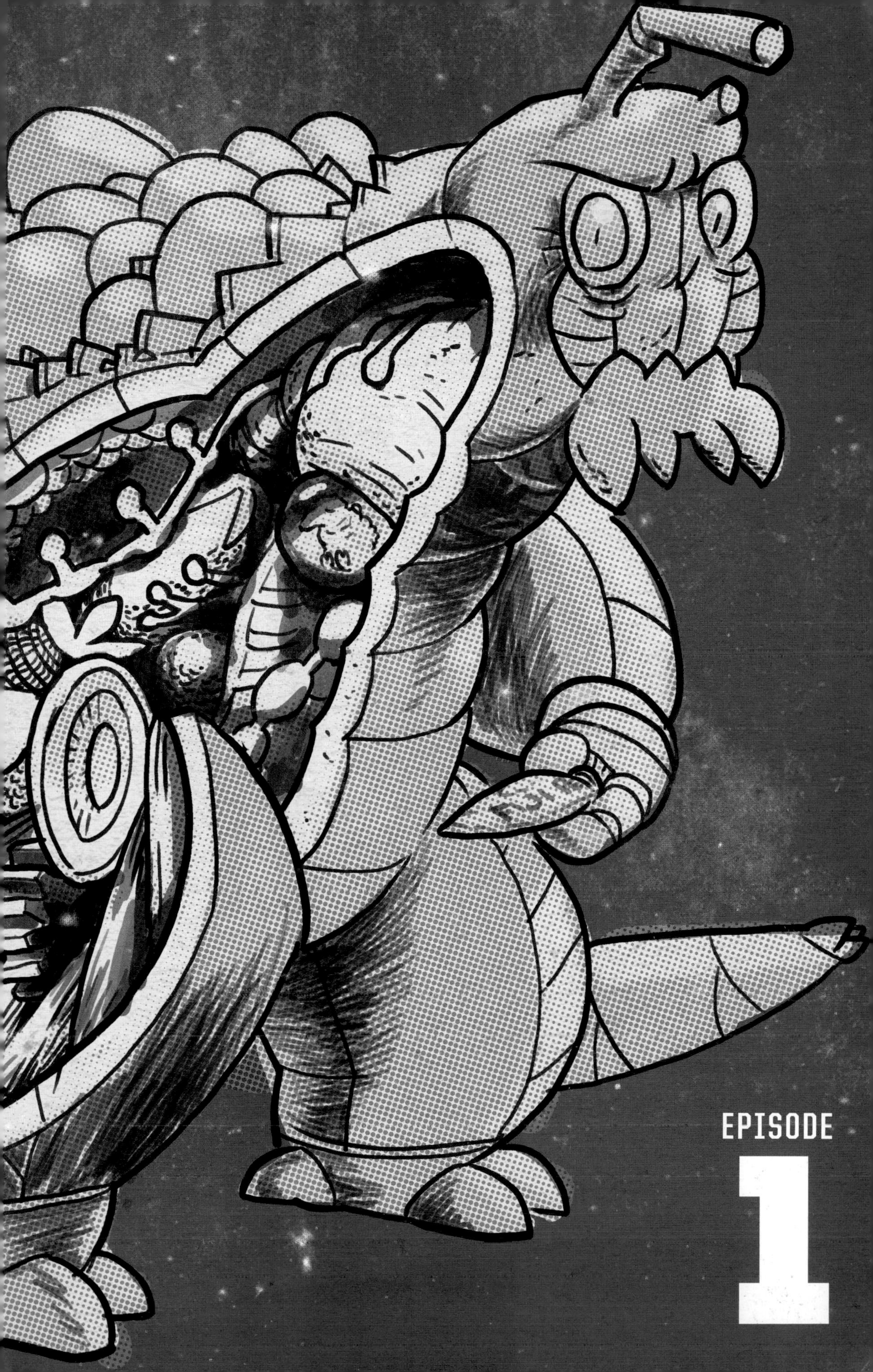
EPISODE
1

圣獣マックス

ZZZz

BBEEPBEEPB
Snerk

BEE
RRR
Nnf

CRIK
WIND CO.

SCRAAPE
WIND CO.

GIFTS

COMPLIANT
怪獣

BBRING

HELLO?
Oh, ah... yes, Boss, I just about to have uh... FIRSTMEAL.
NOW? But work not START for another--
Oh, uh, SURE. Th-that OKAY.

I be right ***IN***.

RESTAURANT

NEWS

NEWS

SAME AMBERGRIS, DIFFERENT DAY

LIZZA, WILL YOU **SHUT UP** AND REDKING LET US **IN??**

DEFCON TWO IS HOW I'M DOIN', MEGAFAUNA! WHAT DO YOU THINK?
YOU TWO SPAWNS OF BITCHES AIN'T WELCOME HERE, YOU FEEL ME?
I'M ON GOJ-DAMNED PAROLE! THEY FIND OUT I EVEN TALKED TO YOU, MY TAIL END IS BACK IN K-MAX, NO QUESTIONS ASKED!
YO, MON, WE KNOW. WE IN THE SAME SITUATION.

LIKE DARVAZZA YOU ARE. YOU'RE FUGITIVES.
I'VE GOT A GOJ-DAMNED STRAIGHT JOB AND I'VE BUILT A GOJ-DAMNED STRAIGHT LIFE AND YOU TWO JAIL-BIRDONS ARE ABOUT TO FLUSH IT DOWN THE GOJ-DAMNED VOLCANO.
SO YOU AND YOUR BOY CAN TURN AROUND AND ROOSTER-TAIL IT ON BACK TO THE OCEAN.
WHOA, WHOA, BRO.

IT DON'T HAVE TO BE LIKE THAT, YO.
LISTEN, DON'T WORRY ABOUT THIS GUY. HE'S ALL BURNIN' TO GET TO HIS KIDS UP IN THE STRAIT. HE'S LEAVIN' TONIGHT.
AIN'T THAT RIGHT?
YEAH.
BUT YOU AND ME? WE GOTTA TALK ABOUT THIS STRAIGHT JOB, MON.
I MEAN, WE HAD THIS TOWN ON LOCK BACK IN THE HEISEI, KNOW WHAT I'M SAYIN'?

IT'S GONNA BE LIKE OLD TIMES, RED.
BUT--
SH-SHH. I MEAN, BRO, GETTIN' THE HUMONGOS BACK TOGETHER?
YOU KNOW THE OLD CREW GONNA BE ALL ABOUT THAT AMBER-GRIS, LIZZA.
WE HIT UP GONDA, KUMAGON, AND GO-GO SPACE BABY, AND WE GET US A HUSTLE AGAIN, YOU FEEL ME?

NO! MARIANAS NO! I SAY SMOOTH WHITE BALLS TO THAT.
I NEED TO GET SUCKED BACK INTO THAT LIFE LIKE I NEED A HOLE IN THE HEAD.
THE OLD CREW? I SAW 'EM. YOU KNOW WHAT THEY'RE DOIN'?

GONDA'S REDKING DEAD.
KUMAGON GOT GRABBED UP BY THE HEAT. LOST AN EYE AND A DORSAL FIN FOR HIS TROUBLE.
AND GO-GO SPACE BABY? YEAH. I SAW THAT SHORTY OUT IN THE BAY.
SNEAKIN' IN THE HARBOR AT NIGHT, LICKING THE SHIPS' HOLDS, TRYIN' T'GET ANY TOXINS SHE CAN.

DIDN'T EVEN RECOGNIZE ME. SO CAUGHT UP IN GETTIN' HIGH SHE DON'T KNOW HER OLD BOYFRIEND.
THE CREW'S GONE, YO. THAT'S WHAT THE MONSTA LIFE DOES. IT'S--
TOTALLY.
I HEAR WHAT YOU'RE SAYIN', YO.
SO ALL WE GOT TO DO IS PUT THE WORD OUT, AND NEW MEGAFAUNAS'LL BE LININ' UP RIGHT--

GOJ DAMN IT!
YOU DON'T SEE. YOU'LL NEVER SEE. JUST FORGET IT.
I GOT TO GO TO REDKING WORK.

YEAH, SO, UH...
LISTEN, FRIEND. SO WE'RE CLEAR, I'M OUT OF HERE AS SOON AS IT'S DARK AND THE SKIES CLEAR.
YOU DON'T WANT THEM SPOTTING ME COMING OUT OF HERE, PUTTING THE HEAT ON YOU.

YEAH. YOU'RE RIGHT. THANKS FOR PUTTING ME IN THAT POSITION, BY THE WAY.
SO STAY HERE FOR THE DAY. SHUT YOUR MOUTH. STAY AWAY FROM THE WINDOWS. KEEP OUT OF MY STUFF.
I'M HOME FROM WORK AT 1900 HOURS. IT'S DARK BY THEN.

I WANT YOUR WORTHLESS MONVICT ASS GONE, OR THERE'S GONNA BE SOME FINAL WARS HAPPENING UP IN HERE, AND I AIN'T PLAYIN'.
COOL.
HARD LUCK, ELECTROGOR. YOU KNOW HOW IT IS THOUGH.

NOT SO FAST, BROTHER.
THAT AMBERGRIS GOES DOUBLE FOR YOU.
DEAREST BROTHER, I MISS YOU.

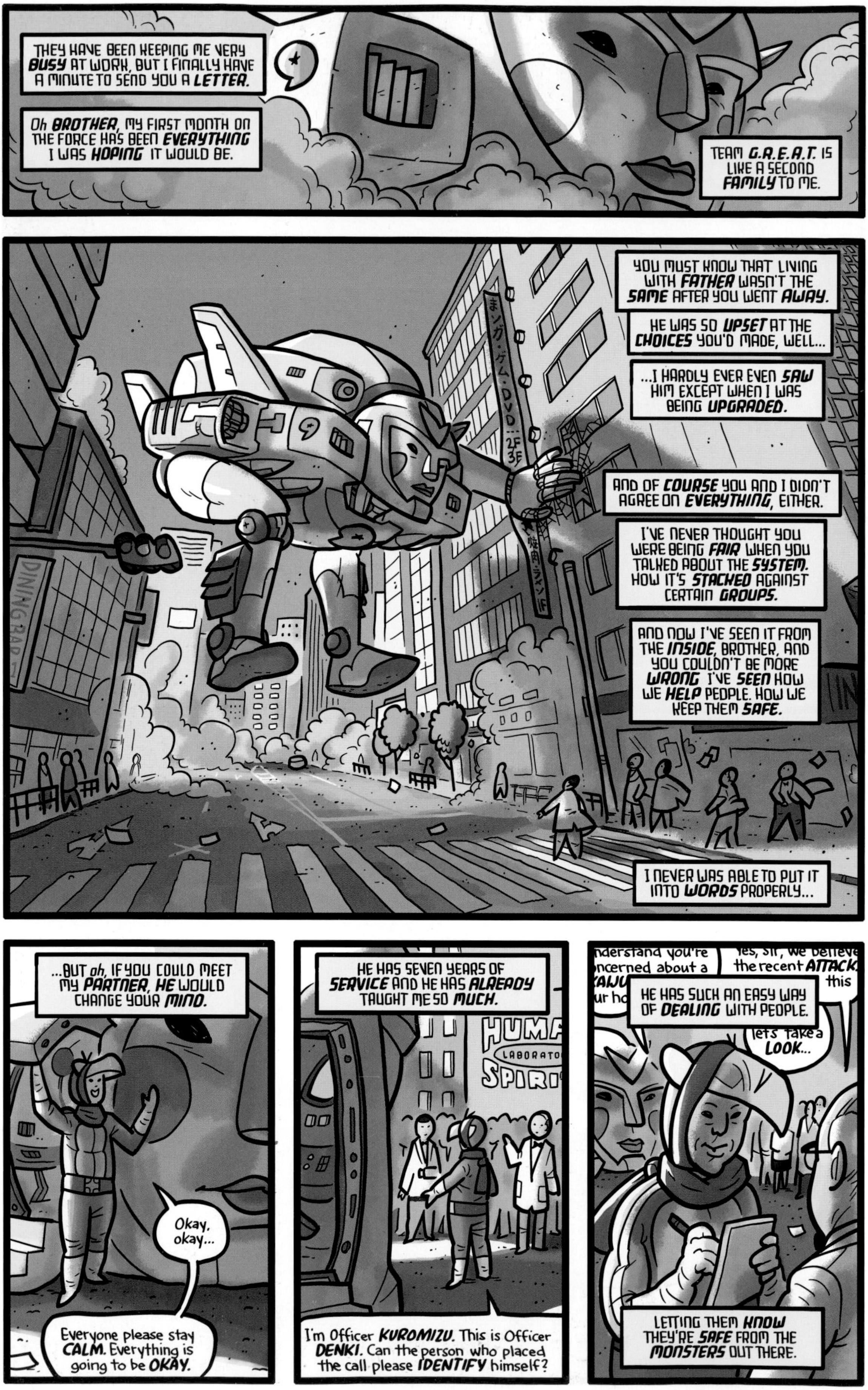

THEY HAVE BEEN KEEPING ME VERY **BUSY** AT WORK, BUT I FINALLY HAVE A MINUTE TO SEND YOU A **LETTER**.
Oh **BROTHER**, MY FIRST MONTH ON THE FORCE HAS BEEN **EVERYTHING** I WAS **HOPING** IT WOULD BE.
TEAM **G.R.E.A.T.** IS LIKE A SECOND **FAMILY** TO ME.

YOU MUST KNOW THAT LIVING WITH **FATHER** WASN'T THE **SAME** AFTER YOU WENT **AWAY**.

HE WAS SO **UPSET** AT THE **CHOICES** YOU'D MADE, WELL...

...I HARDLY EVER EVEN **SAW** HIM EXCEPT WHEN I WAS BEING **UPGRADED**.

AND OF **COURSE** YOU AND I DIDN'T AGREE ON **EVERYTHING**, EITHER.

I'VE NEVER THOUGHT YOU WERE BEING **FAIR** WHEN YOU TALKED ABOUT THE **SYSTEM**. HOW IT'S **STACKED** AGAINST CERTAIN **GROUPS**.

AND NOW I'VE SEEN IT FROM THE **INSIDE**, BROTHER, AND YOU COULDN'T BE MORE **WRONG**. I'VE **SEEN** HOW WE **HELP** PEOPLE. HOW WE KEEP THEM **SAFE**.

I NEVER WAS ABLE TO PUT IT INTO **WORDS** PROPERLY...

...BUT *oh*, IF YOU COULD MEET MY **PARTNER**, **HE** WOULD CHANGE YOUR **MIND**.
Okay, okay...
Everyone please stay **CALM**. Everything is going to be **OKAY**.

HE HAS SEVEN YEARS OF **SERVICE** AND HE HAS **ALREADY** TAUGHT ME SO **MUCH**.
I'm Officer **KUROMIZU**. This is Officer **DENKI**. Can the person who placed the call please **IDENTIFY** himself?

HE HAS SUCH AN EASY WAY OF **DEALING** WITH PEOPLE.
lets take a **LOOK**...
LETTING THEM **KNOW** THEY'RE **SAFE** FROM THE **MONSTERS** OUT THERE.

NO *OFFENSE.*

WE'RE ABOUT TO HEAD OUT ON *PATROL*, SO I HAVE TO CUT THIS *SHORT*.
I *MISS* YOU, BROTHER. I WISH YOU COULD SEE WHAT *I* SEE.
THE *WORK* WE DO. THE PEOPLE WE *HELP*.
STOPPED 4/13
STOPPED 6/21

I WISH YOU COULD *SEE* WHAT'S INSIDE MY *HEAD*.
A morning well *SPENT*, *eh*, partner?
Yeah, you *SAID* it, Chisato. I think we got a pretty good *SENSE* for this thug's *M.O.*
Let's start looking around for some *OTHER* places he might be hiding. We might get *LUCKY*.

"In *ANY* case, Corporal *SINGH* owes us a *ROUND* for this, don'tcha *THINK*?"

GLUP
ANOTHER SAGITTARIUS B2 SPECIAL?

YEAH.
LINE 'EM UP.

SAY, BUDDY, DON'T I KNOW YOU FROM SOMEWHERE?

NO, I DON'T THINK SO, PAL.
NAH, NAH, I THINK I DO! YOU'RE A COP, AIN'T YA?

PRISON GUARD. NOT ANYMORE, THOUGH.
WHAT'S IT TO YOU?
Ohh, A PRISON GUARD. WELL, I WOULDN'T KNOW ANYTHING ABOUT THAT.
I ALWAYS KEPT MY BEAK CLEAN.

I DUNNO. IT'S NOTHING TO ME, IT'S JUST YOU GOT A LOOK TO YOU.
Y'KNOW, WITH THE ARMOR AND STUFF.
L EMPIRE
ASINO

LIKE, "I'LL-BURN-YOU-TO-DEATH-WITH-MY-FOREARM-LASER-AND-DUMP-YOU-IN-AN-ABANDONED-QUARRY" KINDA LOOK.
Mm.

ANYWAY, I'M INFRA-ALIEN GORK. I MANAGE THIS CASINO FOR THE Von VILESTRAS.
YOU GAMBLING TONIGHT?

NAH.
JUST DRINKIN'.
I AIN'T FEELIN' SO LUCKY.
AW, I DON'T KNOW ABOUT THAT. YOU LOOK PRETTY LUCKY FROM WHERE I'M SITTIN'.
STILL IN ONE PIECE, FOR STARTERS.

FORTUNE'S FUNNY, AIN'T IT? ONE DAY YOU'RE FLYIN' HIGH, NEXT, YOU HIT THE OCEAN, AND HARD.
TELL YOU WHAT. HERE'S SOME RAI-STONES. JUST A LITTLE SHUWATCH TO GET YOU OFF THE GROUND, KNOW WHAT I'M SAYIN'?

A LITTLE LUCK.
ON THE HOUSE.

Uh, LISTEN. REAL NICE OFFER, BUT--
UH UH. KEEP IT.
HEAR ME OUT. YOU'RE TOO TALENTED TO BE PROPPING UP THIS END OF THE BAR.

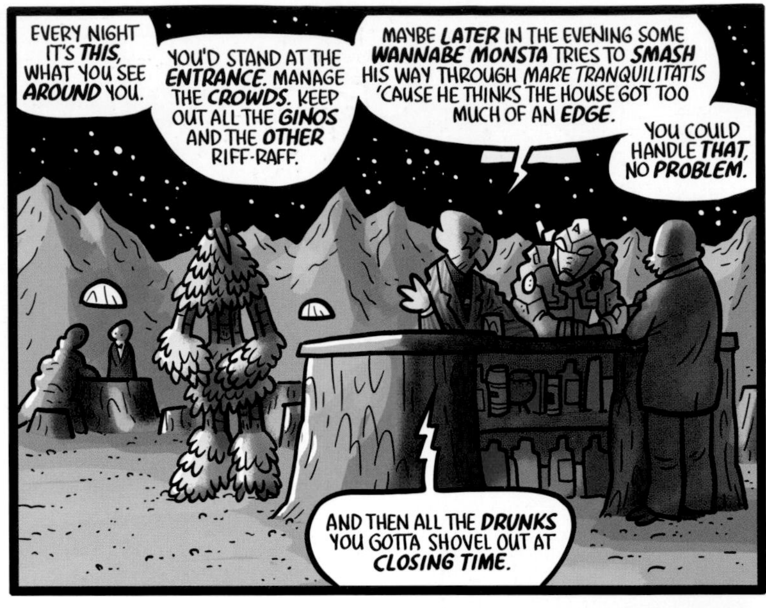
EVERY NIGHT IT'S THIS, WHAT YOU SEE AROUND YOU.
YOU'D STAND AT THE ENTRANCE. MANAGE THE CROWDS. KEEP OUT ALL THE GINOS AND THE OTHER RIFF-RAFF.
MAYBE LATER IN THE EVENING SOME WANNABE MONSTA TRIES TO SMASH HIS WAY THROUGH MARE TRANQUILITATIS 'CAUSE HE THINKS THE HOUSE GOT TOO MUCH OF AN EDGE.
YOU COULD HANDLE THAT, NO PROBLEM.
AND THEN ALL THE DRUNKS YOU GOTTA SHOVEL OUT AT CLOSING TIME.

GOT A COUPLE OF BUSINESS RIVALS, TOO, BUT TAKE IT FROM ME, THIS JOB IS CUSHY.
YOU COULD ASK MY ASSOCIATE OVER HERE, IF HE EVER TALKED.
HEY, WE'VE HAD A LOT O' COPS, LOT O' GUARDS WORKIN' FOR US OVER THE YEARS.
SOME OF 'EM EVEN BOTHERED TO QUIT THE FORCE FIRST.

WHAT DO YOU SAY, KYODAI?
YOU GOT THE MUSCLE, YOU GOT THE ABILITY, YOU GOT THE SMARTS.
READY TO START MAKING THE MONEY?

NAH.
NO THANKS.

YOU CAN JUST SHOVEL ME OUT AT CLOSING TIME.

SERVICE ENTRANCE

DAMN it--
I TOLD you to get here EARLY!
I--
SORRY, Boss-- I got held UP, and coming around to BACK DOOR takes a couple extra--
SAVE it. I don't know WHY I let IWATA-SAN and the PAROLE BOARD talk me into hiring someone I can't even RELY on.
I should have KNOWN, with you SEA-LIZARDS...

Boss, I-I TOLD you a couple TIMES. It my BROTHER who's from the sea.
I was a FERAL CHILD who got IRRADIATED by the--
groan

Excuse ME if I'm not all "BIOLOGICALLY CORRECT" like I'm SUPPOSED to be these days.
Anyway, listen UP. The CRANE broke, so we're moving you over to work on the TOWER.
The "PEACE TO THE FUTURE" fair is only four weeks AWAY, and our HUMAN SPIRIT TOWER is WAY behind.

Okay, so you need me to WELD the sections of the tower to--
NAH.
You're too SLOW on the welding. You're OFF it.
I-I SORRY. I told you my FLAME-BREATHING is not so HOT; it take a little LONGER--

Well, WHATEVER, it's costing us MONEY to have REAL workers do it, so we're taking it out of your PAY.
What YOU have to do, provided you don't screw it UP, is get the PLATES that have the INSCRIPTION and put them on the SIDES of the tower.
We just got them in from our BEST team of TRANSLATORS.
They're out in the YARD.

So I take it you FRANKENSTEIN types can READ well enough to put them in the right ORDER?
Sir, I TOLD you, I not a--
Y-YES, of COURSE. The SCIENTISTS who RAISED me made sure I read very GOOD.
GREAT.

OH, HEY, YO, ZAGURA. WHAT'S UP MY LIZZA?
YOU IN EARLY TODAY TOO, HUH?
I GUESS IT'S THAT MARCH OF PROGRESS THE SQUISHERS ALWAYS BE TALKIN' ABOUT, HUH?

UH, YEAH, GUESS IT IS.
"MY LIZZA."
snicker
WHAT TH'--

HUH.
OKAY, HAVE IT YOUR WAY, ZIPPERBACK.
ha ha ha!
What'd he SAY?

tsk NOTHIN'.
Just LISTEN to him. "Duh, YO, I'm a MONSTA."
"RAAR RAAR RAAR"
HA HA HA
Yeah, "RAAR RAAR"
HA HA! You're all RIGHT, TRENCH-HORROR 2000...

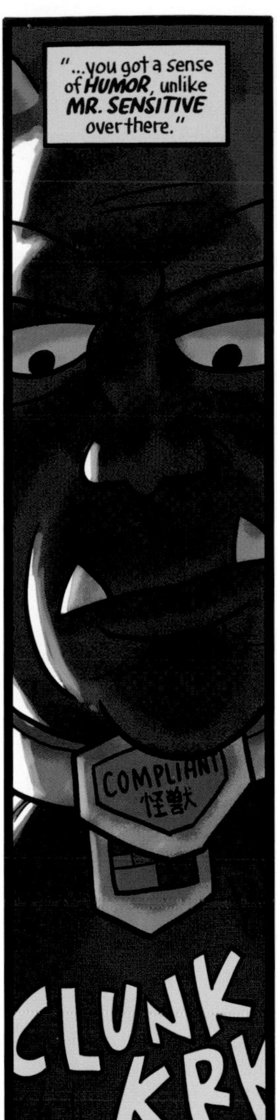
"...you got a sense of HUMOR, unlike MR. SENSITIVE over there."
COMPLIANT 怪獣
CLUNK
KRK

Go! Piercing
forward the
human race
to the
Zero-Kaiju
future time!

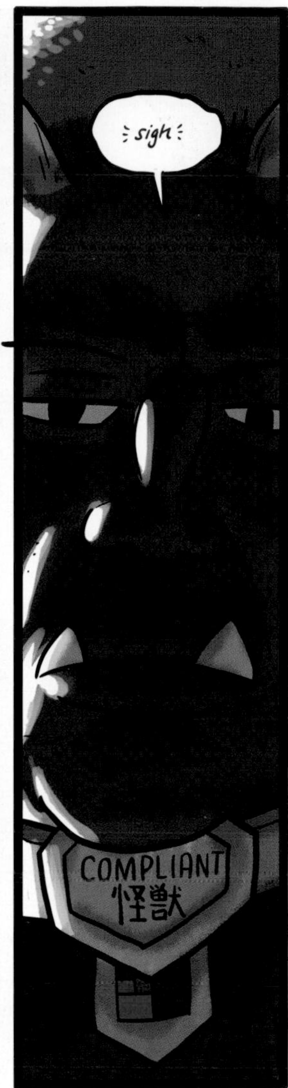
sigh
COMPLIANT 怪獣

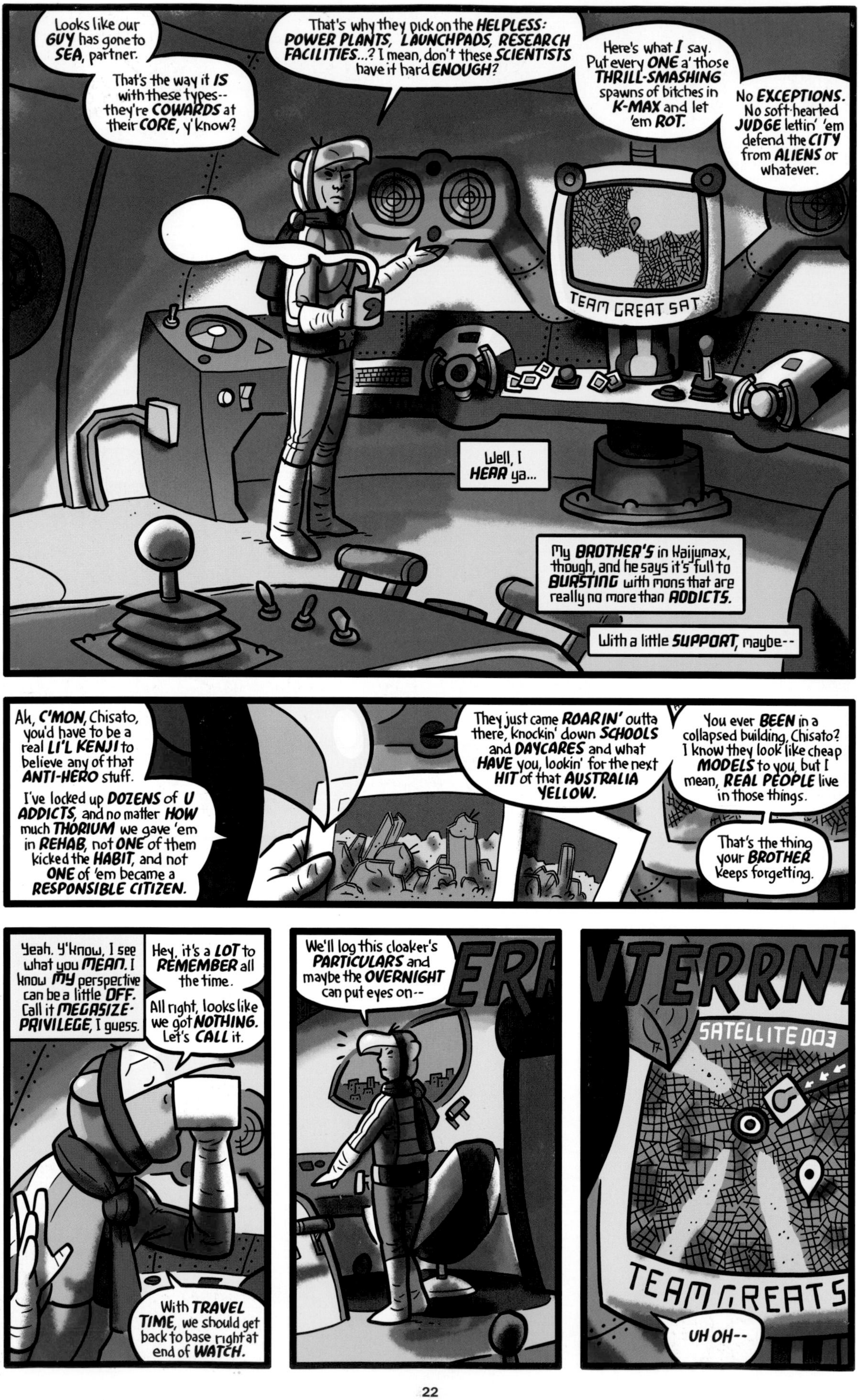

Looks like our GUY has gone to SEA, partner.
That's the way it IS with these types-- they're COWARDS at their CORE, y'know?
That's why they pick on the HELPLESS: POWER PLANTS, LAUNCHPADS, RESEARCH FACILITIES...? I mean, don't these SCIENTISTS have it hard ENOUGH?
Here's what I say. Put every ONE a' those THRILL-SMASHING spawns of bitches in K-MAX and let 'em ROT.
No EXCEPTIONS. No soft-hearted JUDGE lettin' 'em defend the CITY from ALIENS or whatever.
TEAM GREAT SAT
Well, I HEAR ya...
My BROTHER'S in Kaijumax, though, and he says it's full to BURSTING with mons that are really no more than ADDICTS.
With a little SUPPORT, maybe--

Yes, SIR.

Target on INFRARED.

Calculate APPROACH vector.

SOMETIMES IT *IS* JUST THAT SIMPLE, BROTHER.

THAT'S WHAT HOLDS OUR SOCIETY TOGETHER.
THAT ONE BIG IDEAL.
YOU KEEP TALKING ABOUT ALL THE QUESTIONS AND DETAILS AND EXCEPTIONS...
BUT IN THE FACE OF KEEPING HUMANS AND THEIR CHILDREN SAFE...

...ALL THAT LITTLE STUFF JUST FALLS AWAY.

Well, Dr. Katayama, that should put YOUR and your EMPLOYEES' minds at ease, I would think.
It certainly DOES! We can't thank you ENOUGH, Officer!
HAHA!
Not at ALL. We're just doing our JOBS.

AND THAT'S ALL THERE IS TO IT, BROTHER.
I HOPE YOU ARE DOING WELL.
LOVE, Chisato.

Ah.
That TOOK a while.
Is it GONE?
LAB
SAFETY
YES.
Yes, EVERYONE'S gone.

Continue the **EXPERIMENTS.**

GAS
SWOOP
HA HA HA

GOJ DAMN **IDIOT.**
HA HA HA HA HA

HEY guys!
So you heading **OUT**? Like, you gonna go **DO** something? Maybe hang out in the **TRAINYARD**? O-or that big **FIELD**?

Uhh...
Yeah, **LISTEN, TH2K,** I don't know if that's gonna **WORK.**
Yeah, I mean, it's nothing **PERSONAL,** it's just...

"... it's just we're going to do more **HUMAN-SIZED** stuff."

SERVING HUMANS ONLY

KAIJU KEEP MOVING

KAIJU IN BACK

-NO- KAIJU SERVED

"...know your PLACE."
!
WHAT--
RESTAURANT
OH!
Oh, HEY, MON...
NEWS

LISTEN--I KNOW I WAS SUPPOSED TO BE OUT OF HERE BY SUNDOWN. I--
BOTH OF YOU WERE.
YEAH. I KNOW. AND THAT'S THE PLAN. IT'S JUST-- Y'KNOW? THERE'S LOTS OF PLANES AND TANKS AND MASER CANNONS OUT, ALL AROUND HERE. THEY'VE GOT SEARCHLIGHTS AND--

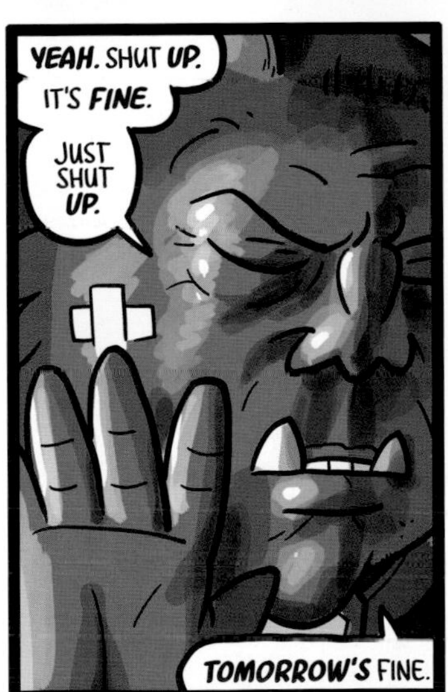
YEAH. SHUT UP.
IT'S FINE.
JUST SHUT UP.
TOMORROW'S FINE.

YEAH, LOOK, THOUGH, AS SOON AS I CAN--
I SAID IT'S REDKING FINE.

CRK

WHAT IN THE GOJ-DAMNED SPACE GRAVEYARD...?
UTSUNOMIYA SH

sigh
zZzZZZz

EPISODE
2

怪獣マックス

KAIJU ENTRANCE IN BACK

WE SERVE KAIJU Takeout only

NO

...and the anonymous tip has placed the kaiju fugitives HERE. That's about HALF A KILOMETER from the site of the upcoming WORLD'S FAIR.
That's an IMPORTANT SITE to the POWERS THAT BE in this city, I don't have to REMIND you.

I need that area SEARCHED. Every DAY they're not FOUND is a BLACK MARK on this CITY and on SCIENCE POLICE TEAM G.R.E.A.T..
GOT it?

These are HARD TARGETS, without much to LOSE. They're not going to come PEACEFULLY.
I want you knocking on every HANGAR DOOR. Be THOROUGH.
Lotta SEASONAL WORKERS there. This is the best place for them to blend IN.

YEAH.
SECOND best, behind that PACIFIC GARBAGE PATCH.
HA HA HA HA HA HA HA HA HA HA

Hey, KUROMIZU, that was a hell of a THING, you taking out that CRYSTAL lizzer yesterday.
HA HA HA HA HA
Oh, yeah, no big DEAL--it was just some SPACE REINCARNATION of a thermo-tweaker we'd already put AWAY.
OR who caught a LASER BOLT in the neck when he tried to ESCAPE...

This is a HIGH PRIORITY ALERT, all of you. Can the BANTER and go to WORK. KUROMIZU, you lead the INTERCEPTION TEAM.
Everyone ELSE, you have your ASSIGNMENTS.
OKAY, hotshots, you heard the COLONEL.
Let's kick the ROTORS and start the MOTORS.

Hey KUROMIZU, how are you liking that new SHIP you got?
Not a bad bucket of BOLTS, as far as THAT goes.
The ETHICAL controls stick here and there, but she's got the POWER where it counts.

Well, you know SLIM and I have got your SIX out there, SEMPAI.
We just have the HOVER-CRUISERS, but we'll be right there WITH you.
THANKS, Pei Wei. I APPRECIATE it.

MAN, this is so much BETTER than working the DOCKS.
All the SOB STORIES, and every strung-out DEEP ONE offering to suck out my INSANITY just to get out of a TICKET.
Yeah, well, none of these BIG BOYS are tryin' to cut a DEAL. You make a mistake with THEM, you PAY for it.
:cheep!:
All right, C'MON, crew...

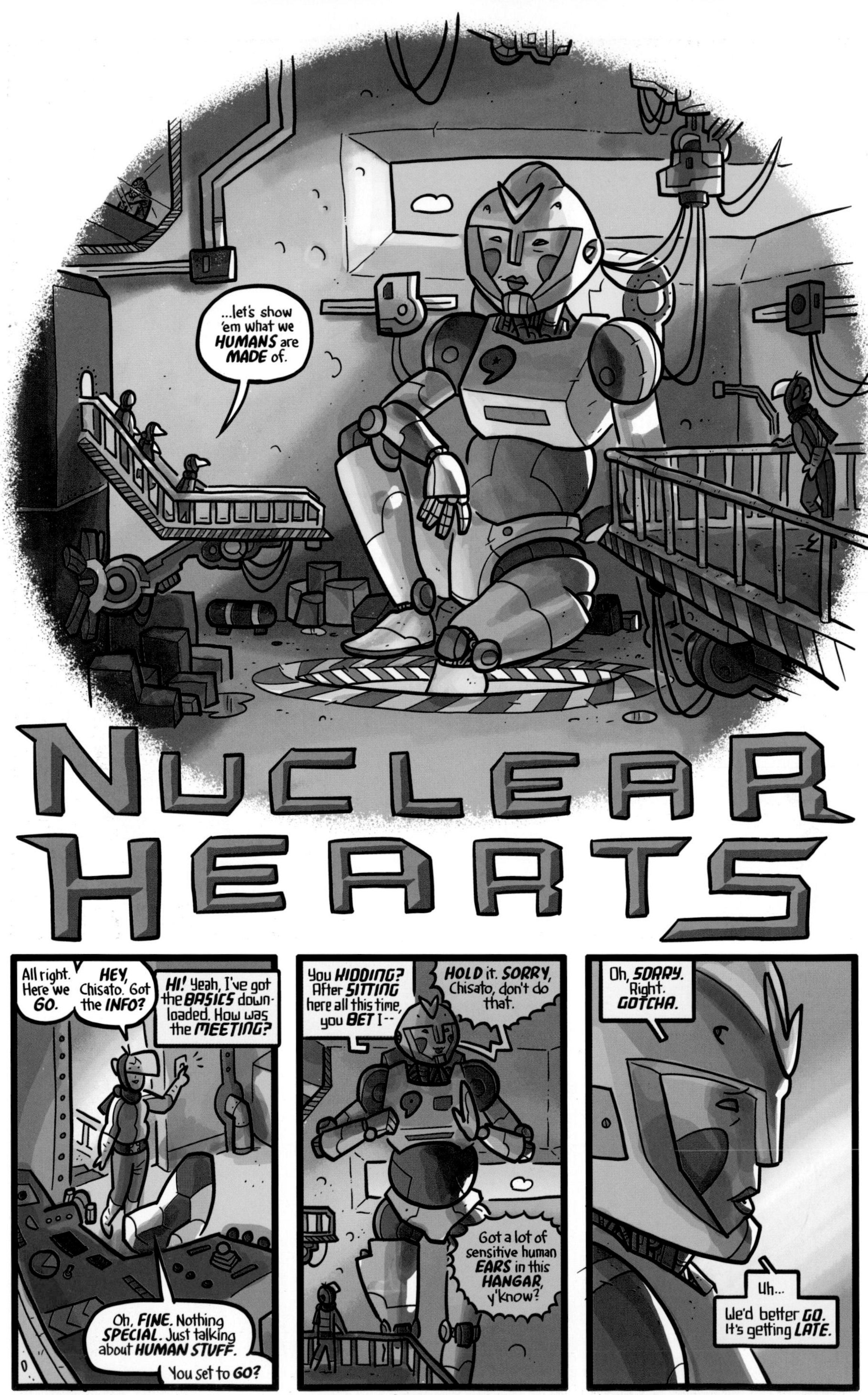

...let's show 'em what we HUMANS are MADE of.

NUCLEAR HEARTS

K-SNERK!

WH--?!

WHAT IN GOJ'S NAME ARE YOU REDKING DOING?!!
GET IN HERE, YOU ZOOKY-ASS MORON!!

WHAT'S UP, MON? JUST GETTIN' IN A LITTLE WAKE 'N' ZAP, YOU KNOW?
SHUT! UP!!
W-WHAT THE HELL ARE YOU--
WHAT DID YOU DO TO MY REDKING ALARM?

OH, YEAH, THAT THING. IT WAS BEEPING IN THE NIGHT, SO I UNPLUGGED IT.
I MEAN, THAT JUST LOOKS LIKE THE SORTA CRAP THE GUARDS WOULD HAVE AT--
WHAT?!

OH MY GOJ.
IT'S GOT TO BE LIKE TEN O'CLOCK!
I GOTTA GET MY STUFF--

I GOTTA GET DOWN THERE BEFORE--
OH, YEAH, THEY CALLED. WHILE YOU WERE ASLEEP.
THEY SAID YOU WERE FIRED.

COME ON, BRO.
THAT JOB WAS GOING NOWHERE.
YOU WANT TO KEEP BUILDIN' THE MAN'S STUFF, MOVIN' HIS FREIGHT AROUND?
THAT AIN'T THE WAY THAT WE CRUSH, YO.
LET ME BREAK IT DOWN FOR YOU.

A LITTLE FOOL TRIP, HE SAY HE OWNS US.
THEN A BIGGER TOOL FLIP, OBEY THE JONESES.

SAYIN' "YESSIR, MISTA SQUISHA, LET ME STEP INTO YOUR HARNESS."
"AND I'LL PITCH UP MY ROAR SO YOU KNOW I'M REALLY HARMLESS."

STOMPIN' AND JIVIN' WHEN YOU COULD BE BALLIN'.
YO.
HOW FAR THE MIGHTY HAVE FALLEN.
YOUR TURN. SHOW ME WHAT YOU GOT, BRO.

YOU THINK I'M GOING TO GOJ DAMN **RAP BATTLE** WITH YOU?
I **NEEDED** THAT JOB, **MEGAFAUNA!** I **HAVE** TO BE **EMPLOYED.** IT'S A CONDITION OF MY GOJ DAMN **RELEASE!**
CAN YOU EVEN **UNDERSTAND** THAT?!

DO YOU KNOW WHAT IT'S **LIKE?**
FITTING **IN?** DOING WHAT YOU'RE GOJ DAMN **TOLD** EVERY GOJ DAMN **MINUTE?!**
DO YOU KNOW WHAT IT'S LIKE TO **BEG** FOR A JOB BACK THAT YOU REDKING **HATE?**

I GOTTA **GO.** I GOTTA TALK TO MY **PAROLE OFFICER.**
MAKE THIS **OKAY.**

THAT LITTLE **SQUISHER** SUMBITCH IS GOING TO COME **HERE** IF I D--

"IT WAS **INEVITABLE**, MAN."

I **KNEW** YOU'D BE BACK. WELCOME, **WELCOME!**
CASINO'S **ALWAYS** A GOOD PLACE FOR A **WAGER**, DON'T YA KNOW. **FOOD'S** NOT BAD EITHER.

THINKING ABOUT MY **PROPOSITION**, HUH? GOOD **MONEY** FOR A **HARD MAN.**
THAT AIN'T IT.
AND AIN'T **NOTHIN'** HARDER THAN STEEL FROM THE **TOMORROW NEBULA.**

ALL THE COPS AN' GUARDS BREAK DOWN **EVENTUALLY**, MY MAN.
MAYBE IT'S A **GAMBLING** DEBT. MAYBE AN **EX-WIFE** SQUEEZING YOU FOR CASH.
MAYBE EVEN SOMETHING AS SIMPLE AS A **BAR TAB.**

BUT THEY **ALWAYS** TAKE THE JOB **EVENTUALL--**

VEET
TARGETING
LOCKED
04
5.56m
DON'T.

S-SEE?!
NOW THAT'S THE STUFF WE NEED AROUND HERE, MAN!
LITTLE FLEXING TO MAKE THE COMPETITION KEEP THEIR DISTANCE, Y'KNOW?

EVERYONE NEEDS TO KEEP THEIR DISTANCE.
I'M JUST HERE TO DRINK.
"I thought you'd be DIFFERENT. I really DID."

But still I get that CALL, don't I?
That one of you has SCREWED UP yet again. Another god damn NO SHOW at work.

It's like I can't get AHEAD with creatures like you. No sooner do I get some damn LIZARD settled into a JOB, then I find out he's off on the WEEKENDS popping NUKE FLASKS at the CONTAINMENT FACILITY.

It's almost like you're INFANTS. 30-story INFANTS.
You think the WORLD is just there as your PLAYGROUND, don't you?

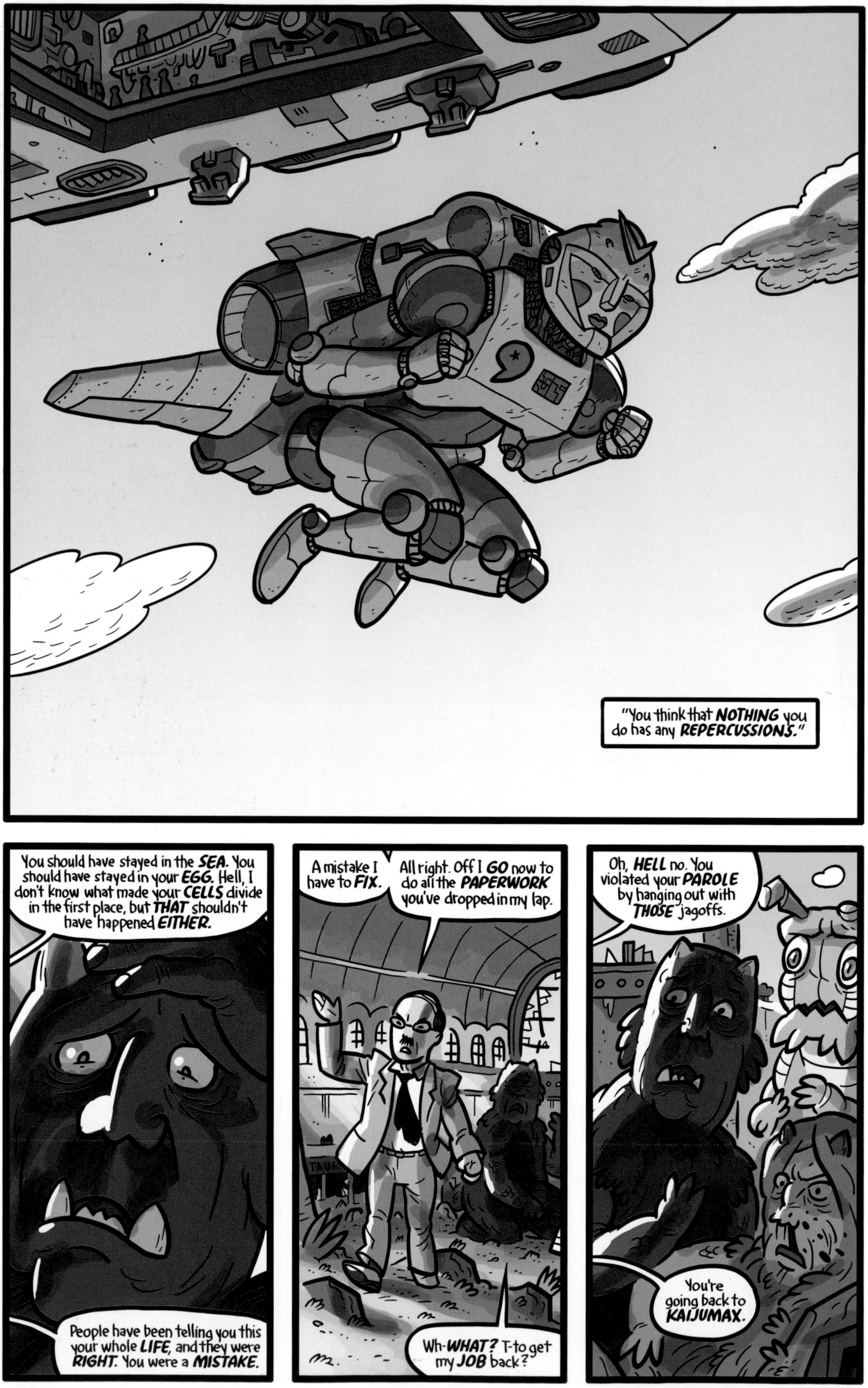

"You think that **NOTHING** you do has any **REPERCUSSIONS.**"

You should have stayed in the SEA. You should have stayed in your EGG. Hell, I don't know what made your CELLS divide in the first place, but THAT shouldn't have happened EITHER.
People have been telling you this your whole LIFE, and they were RIGHT. You were a MISTAKE.

A mistake I have to FIX.
All right. Off I GO now to do all the PAPERWORK you've dropped in my lap.
Wh-WHAT? T-to get my JOB back?

Oh, HELL no. You violated your PAROLE by hanging out with THOSE jagoffs.
You're going back to KAIJUMAX.

Oh, and one **MORE** thing, while I'm on the **SUBJECT**...

SQUISH

SO **THAT'S** HOW IT'S GONNA GOJ DAMN **BE**.

...AND NOW IT'S TIME TO GET **WOKE.**

And we're **DOWN.** Maintain your present **HEADING,** Chisato. We're closing the gap in **30 SECONDS.**

Hmm. You must've hit the ground a little **HARD.** The **TELEMETRY** we're getting from the site is **WAY** off
BAM BAM

It's showing the height as **45 STORIES HIGH.**
That's **TWICE** what **EITHER** of our **FUGITIVES** are supposed to be.
UNSUB
高:150m
重量:90Ktons
♥:2

Maybe the--
Oh **GOD.**

HHUFF

Chisato, TURN!

Pei Wei and SLIM -- break OFF!
This isn't K-MAX'S FUGITIVE! Hang BACK. We don't have any INTEL on this one.

HHRHHH
I'm putting the call in to HQ.

We're going to need the BIG GUNS. Let the G.R.E.A.T ORBITAL LASER take care of this.
Hold on. WAIT. He's slowing DOWN.
Let me TRY something here.

YOU THERE! EXCUSE ME!
WE JUST NEED TO ASK YOU A FEW QUESTIONS.

Uh...
WE'VE HAD A CALL. A FUGITIVE FROM KAIJUMAX HAS BEEN REPORTED IN THE AREA.
WE'RE GOING TO NEED YOU TO COME WITH US.

YEAH?
I'D DEFINITELY KNOW ALL ABOUT IT, WOU
I? SOME SHIFTL
LIZZER STAND
AROUND?
WHO DON'T EVEN KNOW WHERE HE DON'T BELONG?

NO. LISTEN, SIR. THERE'S BEEN A CALL. ESCAPEES FROM--
CHISATO, he's ADVANCING. Draw your WEAPON and take him DOWN.
Hold ON.
Hold ON!
YOU TALKING TO ME?

NO, LOOK. YOU STAY THERE. WE JUST WANT TO ASK YOU SOME QUESTIONS.
ONE OF THE FUGITIVES IS A SEA LIZARD, JUST LIKE YOU. YOU MATCH THE PROFILE. SO IF YOU'VE SEEN--
MATCH THE PROFILE?

I'LL TELL YOU WHAT PROFILE I MATCH, LITTLE MOBILE SUIT...
THE PROFILE O
SOME GREENSKI
COME UP FOR A
AND GET SHOT B
FIFTY BIPLANE
THE PROFILE OF SOME POOR SPAWN OF A BITCH WHO DON'T SIGNAL WHEN HE GO THROUGH DOWNTOWN AND GE
HIS ASS NUKED FROM ORBIT

THE PROFILE OF TWENTY OTHER LIZZAS WHO GOT BOMBED, DRILLED, AND RIDDLED WITH TRACERS WITHOUT SO MUCH AS A "FREEZE, MEGAFAUNA!"
CHISATO.
Take him DOWN, NOW.
NO. I am WORKING this OUT.

SO YEAH, I MATCH THAT PROFILE.
SIR, THAT IS CLOSE ENOUGH.
YOU RESEMBLE A KNOWN FUGITIVE, AND YOU ARE IN HIS LAST KNOWN WHEREABOUTS.
THIS IS POLICE BUSINESS, AND YOUR SAFEST BET HERE IS TO COMPLY.

LET ME TELL YOU WHAT MY "SAFEST BET" IS.
I AIN'T COMPLYING. I AIN'T GOING ANYWHERE WITH YOU TO GET A TUNGSTEN ROD TO THE BACK OF THE HEAD WHEN THE EYE IN THE SKY BLINKS.
CHISATO, take him OUT!
KUROMIZU, shut UP!!

AND I AM THROUGH DOING WHAT SOME SQUISHER SAYS, SOME SQUISHER WHO AIN'T NEVER BEEN IRRADIATED, WHO AIN'T NEVER EVEN BEEN TO THE BOTTOM OF THE SEA.
GET ME?
SIR, YOU TAKE THAT CLAW OUT OF MY CHEST, RIGHT THIS SECOND.

AND I AIN'T DOING WHAT YOU SAY, EITHER, MOBILE SUIT.
SO THAT'S IT. WHAT DO YOU GOT?

SELF-DEFENSE MANEUVER RA6
ARM LOCKED
BALANCE SHIFT +3
TARGET LOCATION CLEAR OF CIVILIANS

HOLD it, Chisato.
INTERRUPT.
Switching to MANUAL.

But--
Reversing LEG TURBINES.

KHRACK

ALL RIGHT!

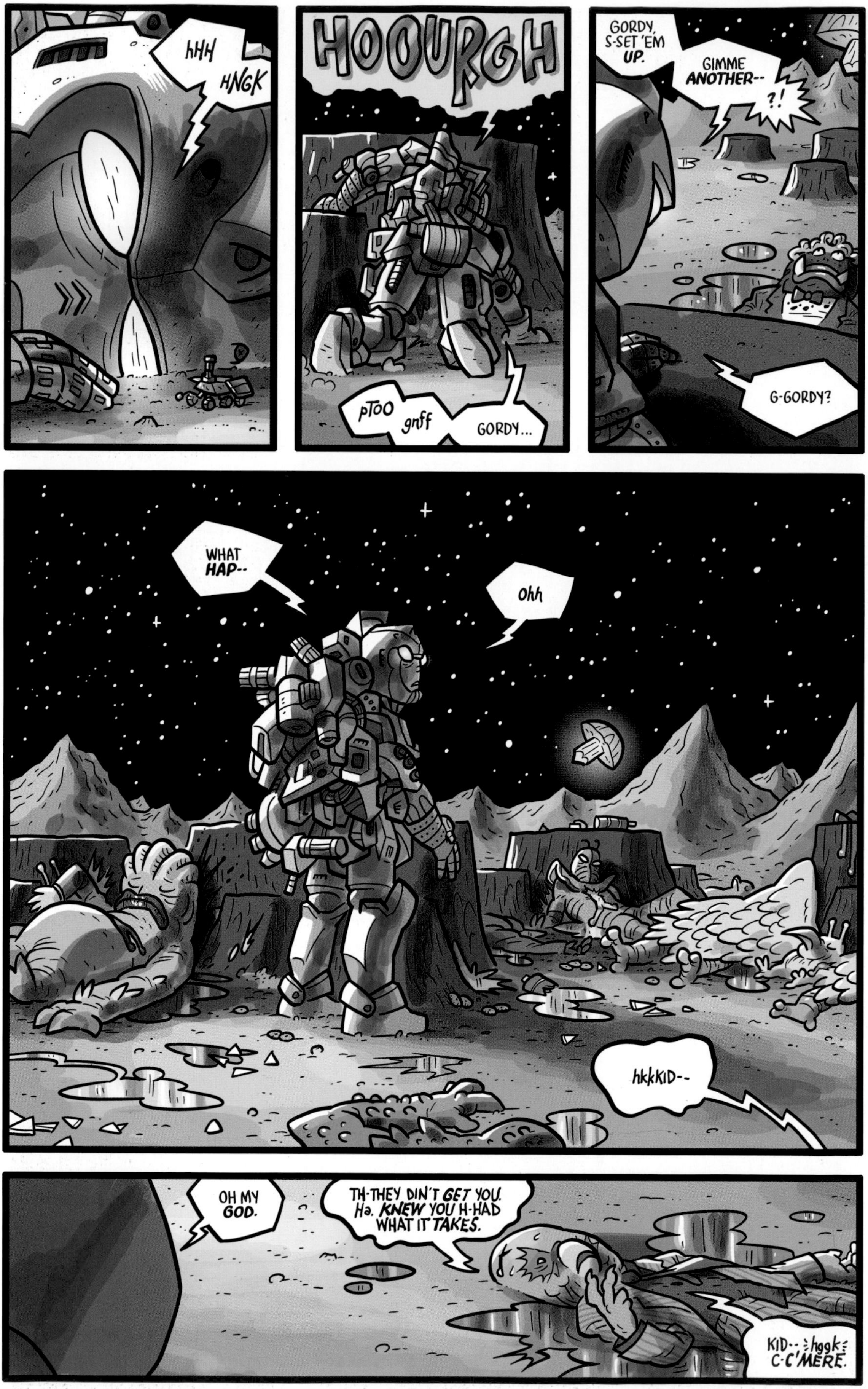

WHAT **HAP**--

Ohh

hkkKID--

LAGOS TRIAD. THEY hgk GOT ME GOOD. HA.
I-IN THE OFFICE. HEALING CRYSTALS. PURPLE.
I-IN THE DUMPSTER. QUICK.

OH MY GOD.
YEAH. YEAH.
OKAY, I'M GOING.

WHERE'S THE--
OKAY.

PURPLE. PURP--
?!
WHAT--

WHAT'S CHAINED TO THE BACK OF--

K-KID, YOU GOT IT.
:hgk: KNEW YOU WOULD. Y'GOT WHAT IT T-TAKES.
WH--
WHAT'S WRONG?

YOU ATE HIM.
WH--?

HE WAS MY #%$!ING FRIEND AND YOU ATE HIM.

WH-WHAT ARE YOU DOING--?
CHOONK

THUNT
NO--

K-KID, PLEASE--

KIIID!!
"No, I don't know his name, do YOU?"

I'm putting his STATS into the ARREST wiki.
Hmm. Looks to ME like it could be PSYCHO WOLF or KURANPASU, only it's too BIG.
Yo, SEMPAI! Nice FINISHING move!
Yeah, ha. THANKS, Pei Wei.
No, SERIOUSLY. You NAILED him! No fancy ARM-LOCKS, just a KNEE to the FACE.

HOLD on, guys. Look at THIS. The BLACK HUMONGO, or, uh, HUMONGO X.
Major PLAYER, but not seen since the NINETIES.
skrk Sempai, this is SLIM.
The guy from the WORLD'S FAIR building -- what's LEFT of it -- he says he had a lizard employee called the RED Humongo.

WAIT-- RED?! Isn't the GREEN one our FUGITIVE?
Oh, for CRYING out-- Hell with THAT.

Close ENOUGH.
ALL

Okay, let's get this one BACK to--
WAIT a sec. CHISATO, did you put SHOWA cuffs on him?
Yeah, WHY?
C'mon, this guy's MILLENNIUM. You need the TOMORROW NEBULA steel ones. It's REGULATION.

Right, SORRY. GOT it. I'll SWITCH 'em.
Guess I got a little AMPED.
I-I feel like I was trying to talk SENSE to him, but he WOULDN'T--

Don't WORRY about it. These guys, they're born APEX PREDATORS. No EMPATHY.
We can TALK and TALK about what MADE them that way...
...but FIRST we've got to bring 'em to HEEL.

And at the end of the DAY...
Go! Piercing forward the human race to the Zero Kaiju future time.
You just never KNOW what will set someone OFF.

All right, you ready to get this half-assed FRANKENSTEIN back to HQ?
YEAH, let me just get--
Dammit, NO--

SEMPAI--PEI WEI here. We've got everything set to GO. Are you--

CRUNCH
SKREEK

Oh GOD. Oh NO.
ch-KEEK!
s-SEMPAI--?

CHECK TO MAKE SURE ANY NEW HARDWARE OR SOFTWARE IS PROPERLY INSTALLED.

BEGINNING DUMP OF PHYSICAL MEMORY.

CONTACT YOUR SYSTEM ADMINISTRATOR.

HUH

EMPAI!!
OME IN,
SEMPAI!
GET THAT
LIZZER!!
OPEN
FIRE!!
DIE!
NO!
SEND BACKUP
ZOOSH
KOOM
BRRTT

MOVING
TAIL
OVER
THERE
NO

NO NO
WATV I
DUN
CLEAR A
PERIM-
ETER
HOLD
YOUR
FIRE
HOLD
POSITION,
WAIT FOR
BACKUP
BRTTT
ZOOSH
LIKE
HELL
WE

10-4
BACKUP
ON THE
WAY
SEMPAI,
COME IN
CIRCLE
ROUND
PLEASE
TAKE
THAT
GET BACK
NO
WATV I
DUN
WHAT
RIGHT
THERE,
RIGHT
THERE!!
TWO
APHRODITE
SIX
HE'S
MOVING
SHOOM
BRTTT
SHOWW
KOOM
FSHHH
SECURE
THE AREA
FIND
SECOND
FUGITIVE

1
2
3
4
EPISODE
3

怪獣マックス

WHOOFY™

APE-WHALE™

Circle AROUND!
We've GOT him! He's backed into a CORNER!
huhh
huhh
n-NO

BLEAT!
MASER'S warming up...
Target the HEAD. That SHELL looks pretty TOUGH.
huhh
NO!

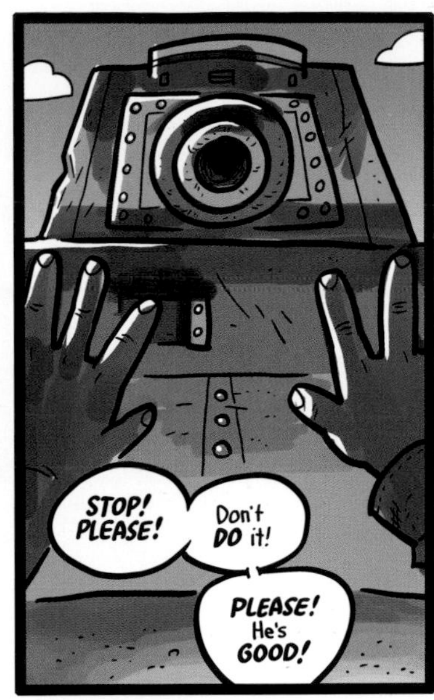
STOP! PLEASE!
Don't DO it!
PLEASE! He's GOOD!

WARDEN?

I made some COFFEE. Want a cup?
I don't know how long you're going to be WAITING out here.
Oh, yes, sure, THANK you, KAMAKURA.

Won't be long NOW. I see her COMING.
This is the big MATSUMOTO meeting, huh?
But it's going to be a heck of a DAY.

Yeah. I was nervous ENOUGH about it BEFORE we had an escape. AND a death, and two GUARDS quitting.
She's going to want an ACCOUNTING for all that stuff if we want our BUDGET approved.

But she's been a PRISON ADMINISTRATOR for YEARS. She knows things just HAPPEN, doesn't she?
SURE, but YOU'VE met her. She's stricter than STRICT. She wants to make things run the way they USED to, back in SHOWA times.

It's just the way she IS.

OLD SCHOOL

Ye-es, I BET. Plied them with extra SPIDER CRAB RATIONS and more YARD TIME, and OTHER perks, no doubt.
Isn't it FUNNY how two inmates ESCAPE, endangering the WORLD, and it's only OTHER PRISONERS that benefit?
It's almost CUTE.
I--

So NO, Warden, I DON'T think I will be getting OUT to walk AROUND with you.
In FACT...
...perhaps you would prefer to sit in my JUMP SEAT...
...and I will take YOU on a tour INSTEAD.

The AIRLOCK should take care of any lingering RADIATION.

KANG, there was a day not too LONG ago when we didn't CODDLE these creatures.
MOST of them didn't MAKE it to captivity. Justice was SERVED right there on SITE.
FFFFFF
ELEGANT in its SIMPLICITY. An EYE for a RESIDENTIAL DISTRICT.

But the powers that BE -- far above MY pay grade, BELIEVE me -- insisted we IMPRISON them instead.
To be FRANK, I think it's all about MONEY, bringing them BACK again and again.
Ah...
I'm sure you're RIGHT, Dr. Matsumoto.

A-All I can say is that attitudes have CHANGED on what IS and isn't JUST.
And it's not always the SAME as what is and isn't SAFE.
TSSS
松本
コックピット
YOU'VE done more to keep us safe than ANYONE...

But not **EVERYONE** can be as **TRADITIONAL** as you.

PLEASE, Chisato, for ME.

Now I'll set this down over HERE.
Come on, honey, up you COME.
KOFF

All right, let's get some JUICE in you, okay?

Thanks

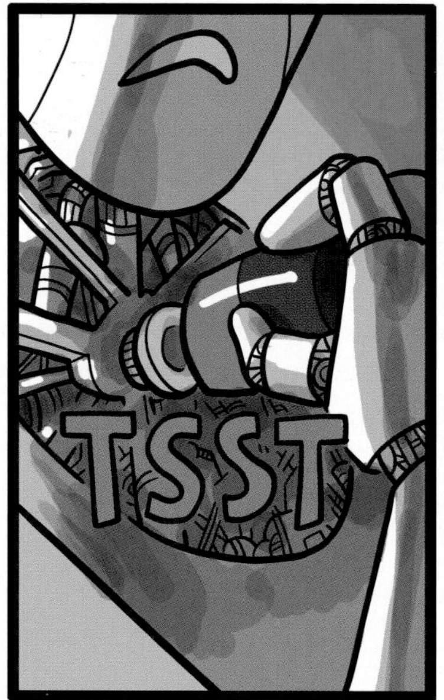
TSST

There, now, doesn't that feel BETTER?
Oh!
Oh, okay, now you REST. GORO and I have to do quite a bit of WORK today.
Yes sir, and don't forget about your TEA.

KOFF
That's RIGHT. You make such a good CUP, Goro.
Oh, it's all in the CEREMONY.
No big DEAL.
Should we get down to our little FRIENDS?

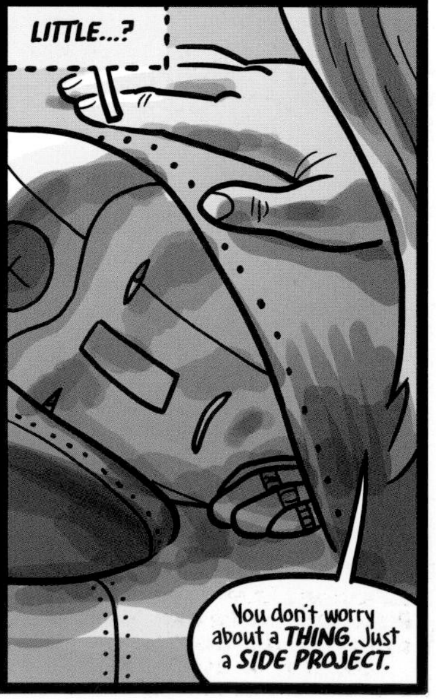
LITTLE...?
You don't worry about a THING. Just a SIDE PROJECT.

You'll always be my NUMBER ONE.
"Grown-ups, please LISTEN to me!"

Destroying this MONSTER is a TERRIBLE MISTAKE!
HEEE
This is not a BEAST from outer SPACE, like those sinister GIGLOGONS, whose flying TOROID SHIPS held the city in a GRIP of TERROR last week...
This is ZUGAIGO, PROTECTOR of ALL ASIA!

GUHURR
ZUGAIGO has saved EACH of our lives from the GIGLOGONS this week!
He makes his intentions KNOWN, i-if only we would LISTEN! If only the WORLD could listen in PEACE, together.
YEAH! That is ALL RIGHT!
HEY!!

BLAST! He's getting AWAY!
Swing the TURRET around-- NO! He made it behind those BUILDINGS!

You darn KIDS with your FANCY TALK need to get out of the WAY and let the ARMY handle this.
That thing's been a MENACE for DAYS and it's up to US to blast it to the MONSTER GRAVE-YARD in the SKY.

Bring those TANKS up here!
There's nothing else that can pierce that SHELL. Tell the PLANES to turn back. They're no HELP here.
And you KIDS--
Go HOME to your PARENTS!

HECK! That is NO GOOD, fellows!!
You SAID it. We didn't CONVINCE them! OKAY, gang, we've GOT to help ZUGAIGO.
And I THINK I've got a PLAN.

"Anyone ELSE remember where the MOTHERSHIP crashed?"
I have to TELL you, Warden...

There are CHANGES afoot at HQ.
This latest ESCAPE has really rattled their CRYSTALS up there.
SOME of those RUBBER SUITS are actually starting to LISTEN to my SUGGESTIONS.

Like WHAT?
For ONE, they're getting PRETTY close to passing an LTF ORDER.
THAT ought to make YOU happy. Get out of the WAY and let NATURE take its COURSE?
NO, Ma'am, that's not what we WANT here.

NO?
No, the LOCK-DOWN is just about to come to an END.
We've got NEW STAFF coming in, and we should be back up and RUNNING in a few DAYS.
A few DAYS?

You must be MAD.
Will you be giving the prisoners all a gentle DUST BATH and a complimentary F-4 PHANTOM to chew on as WELL?
Ma'am, if we let the inmates stew in their own JUICES too long, we get MONTHS of DISCIPLINE PROBLEMS.

We HAVE to return our prison to working ORDER.
We have to heal this INJURY. We HAVE a system. It WORKS.

"WORKS."
You're living in a FANTASY LAND, Warden.
That kind of PIE IN THE SKY thinking is what wipes WHOLE CITIES off the--
NNFF
HM?

JUST a moment, Warden.
TK TAK
WIKI
BOUCHON de RIVIERE
HABITAT: CONGO RIVER BASIN
STREET NAME: M. MBEMBE
CHARGE: AGGRA-VATED LURKING
Yep, I THOUGHT so.

Uh, Dr. Matsumoto, he's out of his CRATER on MY ORDERS. He's--
HEY! INMATE!

HNFF
EH? WHAT DO YOU WANT?
Speak HUMAN. What are you DOING over there? BESIDES getting high.

What's it to YOU? I am, what you SAY eating the HOT AIR. like the WARDEN he ASK me to.
Turn it into... eh, like, NOTHING-AIR. Air that... she don't HURT no SQUISHERS.

HUMANS. They're called HUMANS. And that's not NOTHING-AIR, is it?
That's CARBON DIOXIDE. And it hurt some people the LAST time you breathed it out, DIDN'T it?
HNFF
Ehh... like, I don't... what you MEAN?

What I mean is LAKE NYOS 1986.
That's part of your "TURF" or whatever you CALL it, RIGHT?
1700 PEOPLE. ASPHIXIATED.

Ehh, like, I don't know what you TALKING about, SQUISH-- eh, uh, HUMAN LADY--
Like HELL you don't. You know EXACTLY what I mean, PUNK.
UFF!
OWW!

Dr. Matsumoto-- the LAKE NYOS case is CLOSED. And even if he DID cause it, he's HERE now.
He can't hurt anyone ELSE.
HEY SQUISHA-- WHY'D YOU PUSH ME, HUH?

I SAID speak goddamned HUMAN. You don't even have any EARS, maybe you didn't HEAR me.
YO, I got, what you call, TYMPANIC MEMBRANES, squisher! Why you got to DISRESPECT to me, HUH?
I am eh, minding my own redking TERRITORY, you come and J'ACCUSE? HUH? I redking KILL squishers for LESS.

HMM. The words of an INNOCENT MON, I'm SURE.
Can't hurt anyone ELSE, eh, Warden? Not until he finds a SECURITY HOLE and ESCAPES, right?
I thought when I RECOMMENDED you for this job, you would be WITH me, Kang. To battle for RIGHT against WRONG.

But you've never grown out of that childhood FANTASY, have you? Still making flimsy EXCUSES for CRIMINALS. How all they NEED is a little REHABILITATION.
I WONDER what it WAS in your PAST that made you so SOFT.

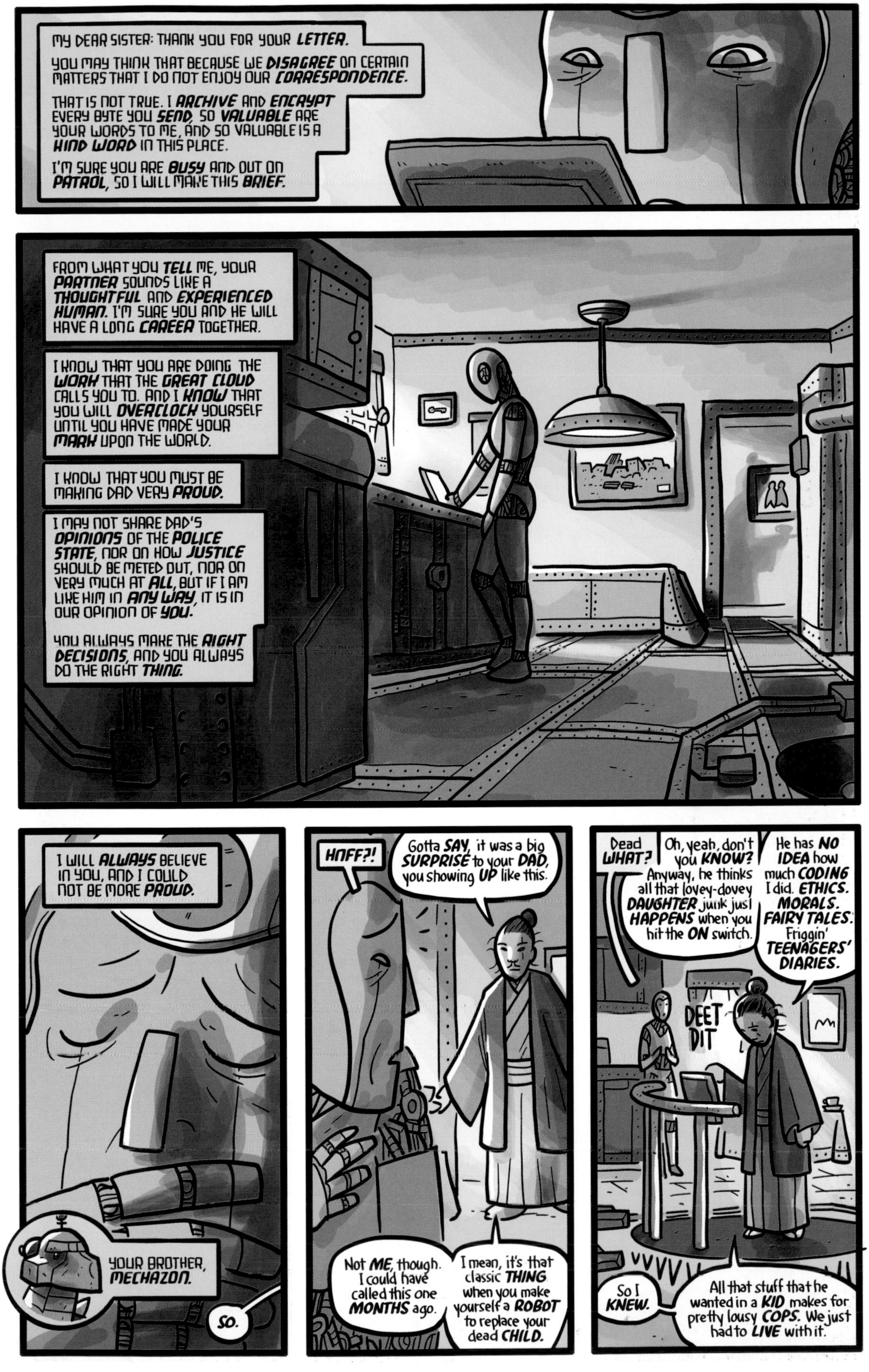

MY DEAR SISTER: THANK YOU FOR YOUR LETTER.
YOU MAY THINK THAT BECAUSE WE DISAGREE ON CERTAIN MATTERS THAT I DO NOT ENJOY OUR CORRESPONDENCE.
THAT IS NOT TRUE. I ARCHIVE AND ENCRYPT EVERY BYTE YOU SEND, SO VALUABLE ARE YOUR WORDS TO ME, AND SO VALUABLE IS A KIND WORD IN THIS PLACE.
I'M SURE YOU ARE BUSY AND OUT ON PATROL, SO I WILL MAKE THIS BRIEF.

FROM WHAT YOU TELL ME, YOUR PARTNER SOUNDS LIKE A THOUGHTFUL AND EXPERIENCED HUMAN. I'M SURE YOU AND HE WILL HAVE A LONG CAREER TOGETHER.

I KNOW THAT YOU ARE DOING THE WORK THAT THE GREAT CLOUD CALLS YOU TO. AND I KNOW THAT YOU WILL OVERCLOCK YOURSELF UNTIL YOU HAVE MADE YOUR MARK UPON THE WORLD.

I KNOW THAT YOU MUST BE MAKING DAD VERY PROUD.

I MAY NOT SHARE DAD'S OPINIONS OF THE POLICE STATE, NOR ON HOW JUSTICE SHOULD BE METED OUT, NOR ON VERY MUCH AT ALL, BUT IF I AM LIKE HIM IN ANY WAY, IT IS IN OUR OPINION OF YOU.

YOU ALWAYS MAKE THE RIGHT DECISIONS, AND YOU ALWAYS DO THE RIGHT THING.

I WILL ALWAYS BELIEVE IN YOU, AND I COULD NOT BE MORE PROUD.
YOUR BROTHER, MECHAZON.
SO.

HNFF?!
Gotta SAY, it was a big SURPRISE to your DAD, you showing UP like this.
Not ME, though. I could have called this one MONTHS ago.
I mean, it's that classic THING when you make yourself a ROBOT to replace your dead CHILD.

Dead WHAT?
Oh, yeah, don't you KNOW? Anyway, he thinks all that lovey-dovey DAUGHTER junk just HAPPENS when you hit the ON switch.
He has NO IDEA how much CODING I did. ETHICS. MORALS. FAIRY TALES. Friggin' TEENAGERS' DIARIES.
DEET DIT
So I KNEW.
All that stuff that he wanted in a KID makes for pretty lousy COPS. We just had to LIVE with it.

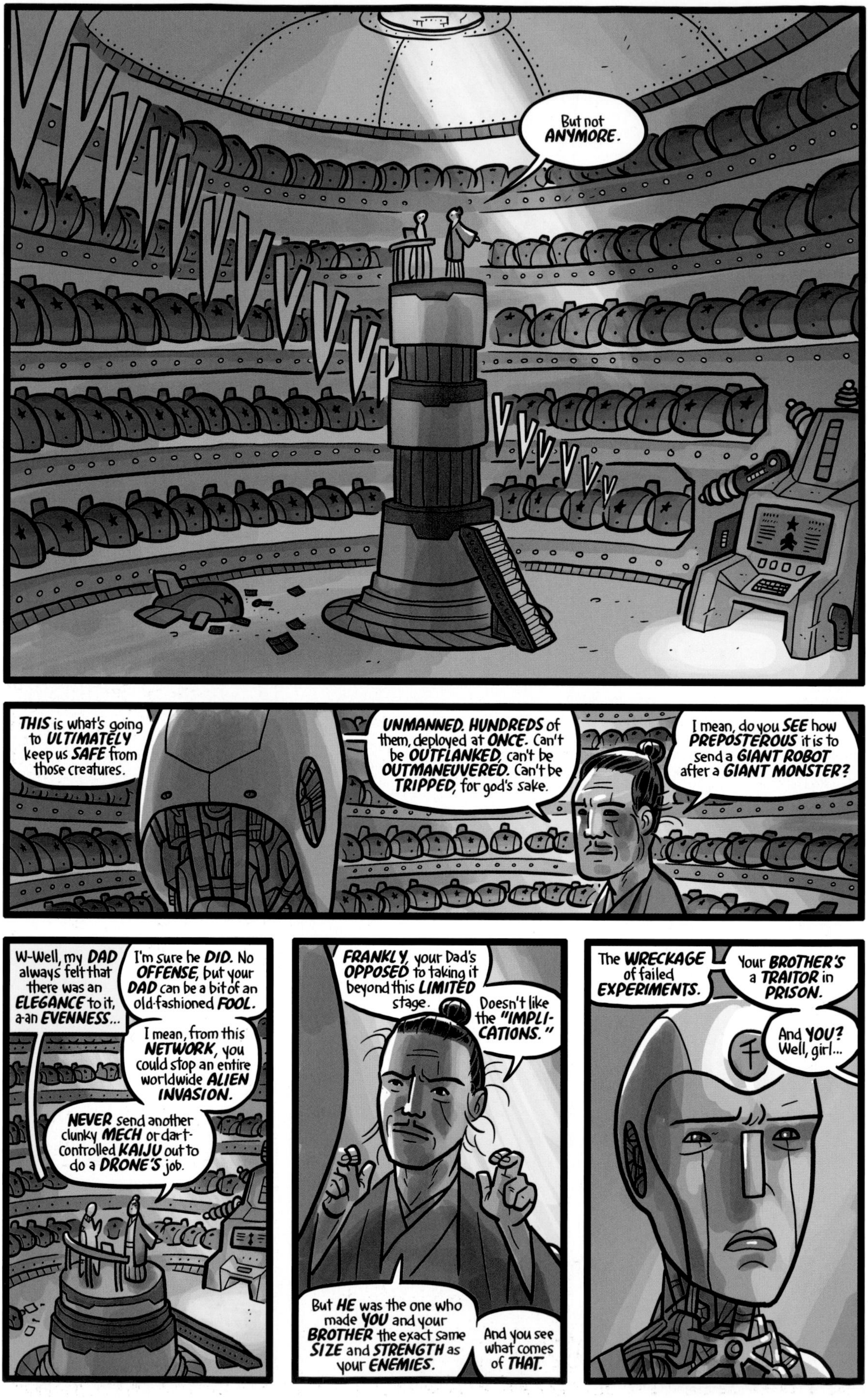

But not ANYMORE.

THIS is what's going to ULTIMATELY keep us SAFE from those creatures.
UNMANNED. HUNDREDS of them, deployed at ONCE. Can't be OUTFLANKED, can't be OUTMANEUVERED. Can't be TRIPPED, for god's sake.
I mean, do you SEE how PREPOSTEROUS it is to send a GIANT ROBOT after a GIANT MONSTER?

W-Well, my DAD always felt that there was an ELEGANCE to it, a-an EVENNESS...
I'm sure he DID. No OFFENSE, but your DAD can be a bit of an old-fashioned FOOL.
I mean, from this NETWORK, you could stop an entire worldwide ALIEN INVASION.
NEVER send another clunky MECH or dart-controlled KAIJU out to do a DRONE'S job.

FRANKLY, your Dad's OPPOSED to taking it beyond this LIMITED stage.
Doesn't like the "IMPLI-CATIONS."
But HE was the one who made YOU and your BROTHER the exact same SIZE and STRENGTH as your ENEMIES.
And you see what comes of THAT.

The WRECKAGE of failed EXPERIMENTS.
Your BROTHER'S a TRAITOR in PRISON.
And YOU? Well, girl...

"...you're **BROKEN.**"
OKAY, I'm trying the **TELEPATHIC IGNITION...**
READY? HNNGH...

Oh, **HEY,** Sis, be **CAREFUL,** don't touch **THAT** one.
LASER
O-**KAY!** Try it **NOW!**

VRNNNNN
Hey, you **DID** it!
ROOTY-TOOT-TOOT!

BULLY!
Here we **GO,** fellows!
Yeah, **YEAH!** Go **THAT** way!
There's a crushed **FACTORY,** right **THERE.**
NO!
THERE he is! I **SEE** him!
Over **THERE,** over **THERE!!**

OKAY. If we can get him to the COAST, he'll be home FREE.
It looks like he's SAFE. He's still AHEAD of the TANKS.
HAA

COME on, ZUGAIGO, you can DO it!!
YEAH, we got your BACK!
SIS-- set the ship to AUTO-FOLLOW. That button THERE. We'll be right BEHIND him, and now we can FINALLY prove to the GROWN-UPS that ZUGAIGO is just trying to HELP.
OKAY!
We LOVE you, ZUGAIGO!

OKAY! Now he's BOSS, MAN!
YEAH, he--
Oh. He kind of CRUSHED that SCHOOL. H-he probably thought it was EVACUATED.
OH!
And that busy TRAIN STATION, too...

Now he's, uh, he's BITING that man's CAR.
No, it's OKAY! The man got out and he's running AWA--
Oh. No, Zugaigo ate him TOO.
I-I'm sure that guy was probably in LEAGUE with the GIGLOGONS...

OKAY! Now he's got a STRAIGHT SHOT to the HARBOR if he would just--
No. He's EATING that bus full of PEOPLE.
And he just knocked over that HIGH RISE.

H-he--
He's the PROTECTOR OF ALL ASIA. He knows what he's DOING.
I know that Zugaigo LOVES us. He has a love f-for the world so DEEP that we can't wrap our MINDS around it.
HEE

The way he EXPRESSES it is just a little--
VLAM

HOLY GOSH!!
WHAT--

Oh, no.
Kenji--

H-he was **HURTING** people...

NOBUKO MATSUMOTO, what is **WRONG** with you?!

Ma'am, PLEASE. It doesn't have to ESCALATE like this. This inmate has been VERY responsive to INCENTIVES. Let me go down and--
Yes, I'm sure you will TALK and TALK, and he will TAKE and TAKE.

And all the VICTIMS are dead and GONE, and we sit around and WONDER if their MURDERERS have comfortable enough BEDS.
LASER

So NO, you're not going to go ANYWHERE, and we're not going to TALK this OUT.
ESTRAIN

ZZRP
WHY--
UFF!
VVVV

EH? YOU IN THERE?
DON'T YOU HAVE A REDKING ANSWER FOR ME, SQUISHER?
YOU JUST GOING TO STAND THERE HUMMING?

WHY, Warden? BECAUSE.
Because we as a SPECIES can't AFFORD to CARE what their INTENTIONS are.
Because the WORLD has GOT to be SAFE.
Because life isn't GOD DAMNED FAIR, Warden.

And SOMETIMES you just have to have the STEEL to do what's NECESSARY.

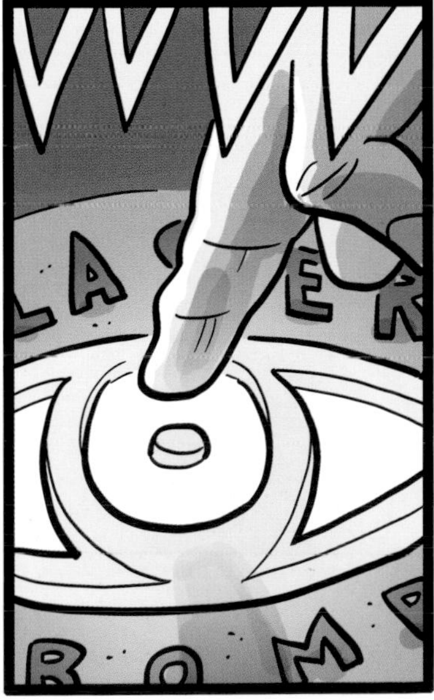
LASER
BOMB

NO.
I'm SORRY, Ma'am--
SHING

KRAK

HNNF! HEY! OW!
THIS IS, WHAT YOU CALL, BRUTALITY OF THE POLICE!
SHUT UP.
YOU'RE STILL BREATHING, AREN'T YOU?

MA'AM, I'M SORRY.
BUT THE WORLD ISN'T BLACK AND WHITE ANYMORE.

EVERYONE'S BEEN HURT.
SO I KNOW HOW YOU FEEL...

...BUT SOMETIMES ALL WE CAN **DO** IS BOUNCE **BACK.**

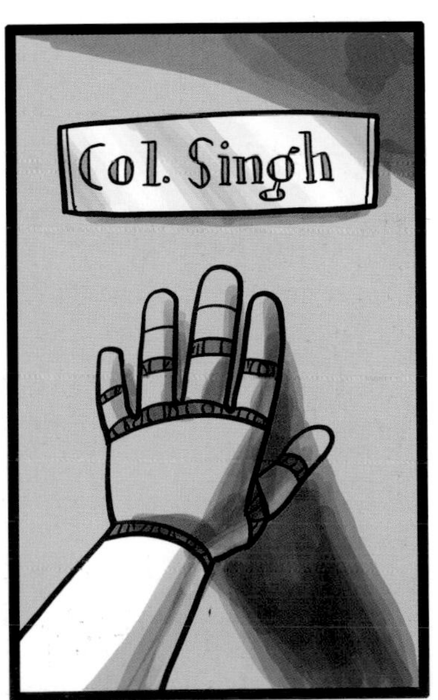

HI.

I KNEW you'd come back to us.

Ma'am, I'm SORRY I took so much TIME to--
I-I just had t-to--
Stop right THERE.
We all need to PROCESS. You GOTTA do it.
That's where WISDOM comes from.
'Least, that's what my new THERAPIST says.

Anyway, you're here at just the right TIME. Got a new ASSIGNMENT for you.
New PARTNER, too.
PARTNER? Okay, well, I look forward to--
Oh, no need to WAIT. He's HERE. Just gotta step OUTSIDE for a minute.

OUTSIDE...?
Aren't we on the...
...fifth FLOOR? YEAH. Come over to this WINDOW and let me INTRODUCE you.

CHISATO, this is JIN-WOOK JEONG.

AM GREAT

交番

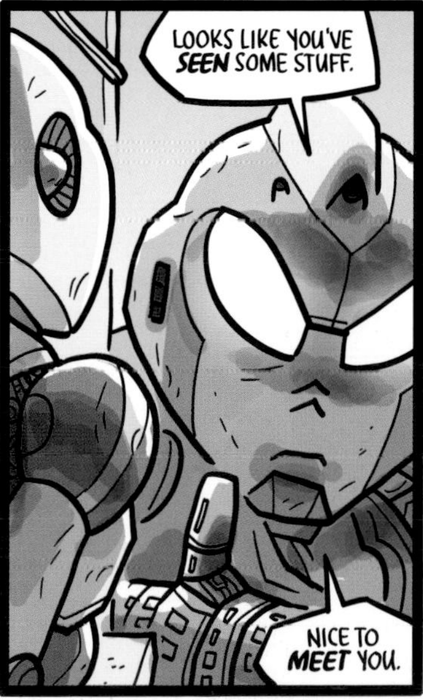

ATTN: COUNCIL OF LIGHT
4th PLANET OF SUPERKING SYSTEM
As per your RECOMMENDATION, I visited Earth's SECURITY SITE 6A, located at coordinates 177 WEST, 17 SOUTH.
Upon meeting with WARDEN JAE-YOON KANG, I went on a comprehensive TOUR of KAIJUMAX PRISON.

Contrary to my EXPECTATIONS, the prison was in good REPAIR...
...and the period of LOCKDOWN instituted in the aftermath of the ESCAPE is now drawing to a CLOSE.

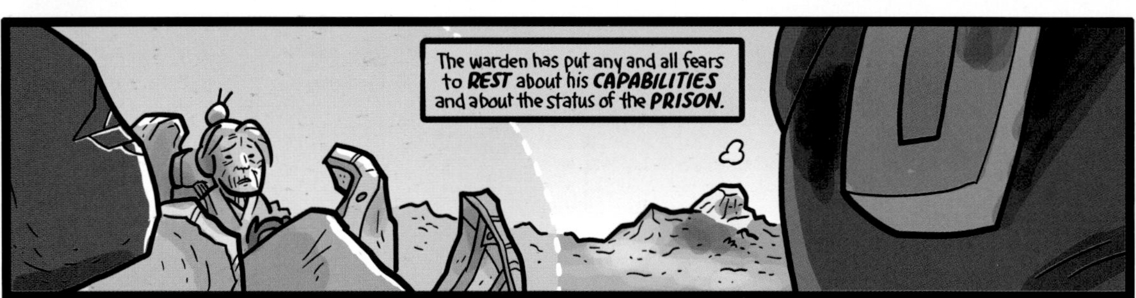
The warden has put any and all fears to REST about his CAPABILITIES and about the status of the PRISON.

As I noted when I RECOMMENDED him for the job, Warden KANG is PARTICULARLY suited to this branch of KAIJU LAW ENFORCEMENT.

In accordance with CUSTOM in the NEBULA OF THE ETERNAL SUNRISE you may now take Kaijumax's CRYSTAL COLUMN...
...and place it upon the "APPROVED" plinth for the upcoming BUDGET PERIOD.

I consider the matter SETTLED.

Rest in peace...

...Zugaigo, Protector of Asia.

yours,

NOBUKO MATSUMOTO

EPISODE
4

怪獣マックス

ALL UNITS-- we are in PURSUIT.
UNKNOWN MONSTER off the coast of REBUN ISLAND.
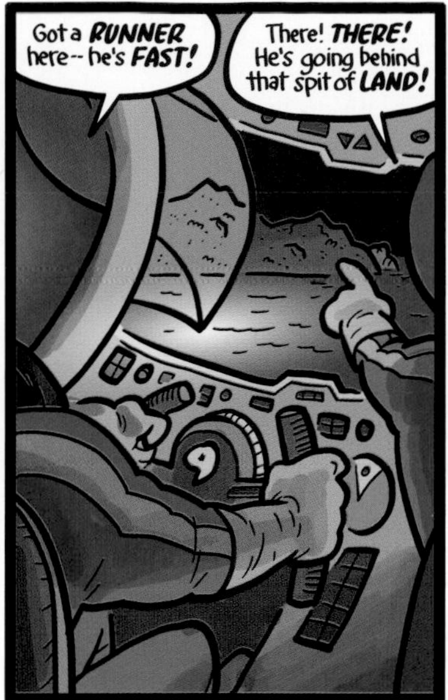
Got a RUNNER here-- he's FAST!
There! THERE! He's going behind that spit of LAND!

QUICK! He's circling back AROUND!
If he makes it to the PROLIV LAPERUZA, he's going to--

NAH. There he IS. Team G.R.E.A.T. SATELLITE has got him.
HHH HH
It's getting him SCANNED. We'll have his STATS up in a MINUTE.

There he GOES again! FOLLOW him!
That sucker just NEVER gets tired! Who IS this guy?
THERE!
THERE! The WIKI'S come up.

HOLY--
[SUBJECT IDENTIFIED]
ELECTROGOR
[CONVICTION: GRAND THEFT ELECTRICITY]
This guy's on the PRBI Ten Most WANTED List!

NO-- He's heading for the CONTINENTAL SHELF!
He's going DOWN!
There! THERE! Sub 43, GET him, you're CLOSEST!
GET him, before he--
NO--

Sub 43, DIVE! DIVE!!
Ah, DAMN it.
Nah, pull BACK, pull BACK.
WHAT?!

No, keep GOING! We can GET him!
TOOM
Nah, LISTEN, man, let him GO. Once you get down below the THERMOCLINE...

"...**THAT'S** when the neighborhoods get **REALLY** bad."

BEWARE of SHOGGOTH

the SEAMY UNDERBELLY

AAH.
YOU KNOW **ME**. NOT MUCH OF A **SOCIALIZER**.
POLICE
交番

I HEARD IT WAS BECAUSE YOU WRECKED **NGUYEN** AND **CHU'S HOVERCYCLES. PLUS** LIKE THIRTY **OTHER** VEHICLES.
WELL, THERE'S **THAT**, TOO.

HA.
ALL RIGHT, I'M GOING TO GO OVER TO THE **HANGAR** AND JACK INTO MY **ME-MECH.**
I DUNNO WHAT WE'LL WANT TO BE **BIG** FOR, THOUGH.
SEEMS LIKE THE **EYE IN THE SKY** HAS IT ALL TAKEN **CARE** OF.

YEAH, I DUNNO, RELYING ON TECHNOLOGY SO **COMPLETELY** LIKE THAT IS **NEVER** A GREAT **IDEA.**
I MEAN, NO **OFFENSE.**
TELL YOU **WHAT.**
I'LL BET YOU **DINNER** THAT **YOU AND I** CAN FIND HIM **FIRST,** EVEN IF WE **ARE** ON VICE.

HUH. OKAY, I'LL **TAKE** THAT BET.
YOU'RE AN INTERESTING **PERSON**, JIN-WOOK JÉONG.
I BET THERE'S MORE TO **YOU** THAN MEETS THE **EYE.**

MAYBE THERE **IS.**
YOU **READY?**

RRRRRRRRR

OKAY, YO, SHH-SHH. TAKE IT EASY THERE, BOY. JUST NEEDING TO REST HERE AND HIDE FOR A QUICK SECOND. JUST TILL THAT LIGHT PASSES OVER.
EASY, BOY.
RRRRR RRR
TEKELI-LI! TEKELI-LI!

EASY, EASY!! DOWN, BOY!
TEKELI-LI! TEKELI-LI!
YO! WHO the FHTAGN is OUT HERE?
AUGGIE! SHUT your HOLE!!

TEKELI--
IPE!
YO!
KRAK
WHO THE FHTAGN ARE YOU?
AND WHAT THE FHTAGN ARE YOU DOING HERE?!

UH, UH, YO, LOOK, MISS, I DON'T WANT NO TROUBLE, YOU FEEL ME? I'M JUST PASSING THROUGH--
WELL, YOU GOT TROUBLE, MEGA-FAUNA! YOU CAN'T FHTAGNING COME IN HERE AND BRING THE FHTAGNING COPS WIT' YOU!!

I DON'T CARE WHO YOU IS, I DON'T CARE NOTHIN' ABOUT YOUR BUSINESS! YOU GO ON AND TAKE YO' ZOOKY ASS OUT MY HOUSE AND BACK TO LAND, MEGAFAUNA!
WAIT WAIT WAIT!
L-LISTEN! I CAN'T GO OUT THERE. PLEASE! THE COPS ARE LOOKING FOR ME. I GOTTA--

I DON'T GIVE A FHTAGN, MEGA FAUNA!! YOU GET OUT THERE, AND I HOPE THEY BLOW YOUR FHTAGNING HEAD OFF!!
G-GOAT...
Y-YO, GOAT...

WHAT THE FHTAGN YOU WANT, NUKE?
DON'T YOU SEE I GOT BUSINESS?
N-NO, I DON'T SEE N-NOTHIN', GOAT...
P-PLEASE, I-I GOT IT BAD, GOAT. I NEED A CRATE, YO. J-JUST A CRATE.

YOU TAKE YOUR BLIND IDIOT ASS INSIDE AND SHUT THE FHTAGN UP!
I TOLD YOU, CUTTLE AIN'T BACK WITH THE STUFF YET!
P-PLEASE, A-ANYTHING, GOAT...
MEGAFAUNA, I'M WARNING YOU--
WAIT!

LISTEN, MAYBE WE CAN MAKE A DEAL HERE, HUH? I GOT SOMETHIN', OKAY?
LOTTA MY ZILLAS, THEY LIKE THIS STUFF.
IT'S U-235. WEAPONS GRADE. IT'S GOOD.
YOU CAN HAVE SOME. ALL YOU LIKE. I JUST NEED ANY OLD PLACE TO LAY LOW.

snicker
HAHAHAHA!
WELL, THERE AIN'T NO PLACE OLDER OR LOWER THAN HERE, MEGAFAUNA, BUT YOU COME PEDDLIN' THAT WEAK-ASS GLOW, AND YOU CAN JUST KEEP ON SWIMMIN'.
N-NO, PLEASE, GOAT... ANYTHING...

J-JUST SOMETHIN' SWEET, TO TAKE THE EDGE OFF.
J-JUST 'TIL CUTTLE C-COME BACK, YOU KNOW...?
YOU FHTAGNING--
FINE, YOU WEAK-ASS NO-NAME FOOL.

GIMME THAT, MEGAFAUNA! TWO OF 'EM!
I DON'T KNOW WHAT YOU PLAYIN', BUT GET YO ASS INSIDE!
G-GOAT, GIMME THAT GLOW...
PLEASE...

SHUT UP! YOU GET WHAT I GIVE YOUR LAND-BEFORE-TIME ASS. GET YOUR FHTAGNING TENTACLES OFF!
AND YOU, YOUNG-BLOOD! YOU STAY PUT. I'M COMIN' IN.
HA. YOU LISTEN TO THAT SHUB OUT THERE, MON...

YOU DON'T WANNA BE WANDERING AROUND. YOU DON'T LOOK LIKE YOU BELONG HERE.
FFP
YOU DEFINITELY AIN'T NO O.G.
BELIEVE ME, I AIN'T STAYING HERE ANY LONGER'N I GOT TO, MON...

"...THIS IS GONNA BE A REAL SHORT VISIT."
...DAD?
Wh-what are you DOING here?
ITING
OOM

KOFF KOFF
KOFF
A FEW reasons.
I'm here to tell you about your SISTER.

CHISATO? What HAPPENED? Is she all RIGHT?
She is NOW. We had to dig her SOUL CHIP out of the WRECKAGE that was her HEAD.
KOFF KOFF
KOFF.
That is, GORO did. As you can SEE, I'm not in the best of SHAPE these days.

B-but she's OKAY, right? She's--
She's FINE. We barely had time to hammer the DENTS out of her MECH before she got back OUT there.
KOFF
She's the COP you NEVER were.

SIGH
Well, thanks SO MUCH for coming by to TELL me that.
I'm glad CHISATO is okay. Now if you'll EXCUSE me, I have to go lead my FOLLOWERS in the morning UPLOAD.
You HOLD it right THERE.

WHY?! So that you can tell me what a FAILURE I am some more?!
How ASHAMED you are of me?!
HUH?
THAT'S why you flew all the way DOWN here, isn't it? CHISATO'S got a goj-damn PHONE.
But you just wanted to twist the SCREW-DRIVER, didn't you?

Y-Your JUDGMENT isn't ABSOLUTE, do you KNOW that, Dad? I don't HAVE to be the THING you created. I DON'T!
You PUSHED me and PUSHED me to be a TOOL of the SMALL MAN.
VEEP
DEET
Enforce his LAWS, protect his corrupt STATE, all by using VIOLENCE against mons just like ME.
You made me into something I HATE, Dad, and I'm redking FURIOUS at you!!

KOFF.
Well, then what are you going to DO about it, you $%#ing COWARD?!
You're ANGRY? Activate those WEAPONS I worked so hard on, then! Blow a HOLE in this god damned MOUNTAIN and turn me into a cloud of irradiated ATOMS!

EYE DRILL #1
UNAVAILABLE
EYE DRILL #2
UNAVAILABLE
KILL BEAM
UNAVAILABLE
POW
UNAVAILABLE
100% MATCH CONFIRMED: CREATOR
DO IT!! What's &%#ing STOPPING you, HUH?
FUZZ BREAKER
UNAVAILABLE
RAIL GUN #1
BATTERY 100%
UNAVAILABLE
MAXIMUM HAND-BLADE
UNAVAILABLE
MAVOLVER
UNAVAILABLE
MULTIPLE VIOLATIONS
L.O.R. #1
P.D. #4
UNAVAILABLE
MELT MACHINE
UNAVAILABLE
LAZOR HAND
UNAVAILABLE
UNAVAILABLE
UNAVAILABLE
VAPORIZER X
LEAF BOMB
UNAVAILABLE
1 2 3 4 5
TAZE

THESE OUT-OF-THE-WAY PORTS ARE WHERE ALL THE SMALL-TIME OPERATIONS COME.

BRINGING IN STUFF LIKE CRATES OF FORBIDDEN ARTIFACTS AND ARCANE TABLETS FROM LOST CIVILIZATIONS AND SO FORTH.

SURE, BUT...

...WHY DO WE CARE? THAT'S ALL LEGAL.

WAIT, WHAT'S SHE--
JUST WATCH.

I CAN BARELY PICK IT UP. SOMETHING ABOUT ... CORRELATING THE CONTENTS OF... SOMETHING...

I SUCKY SUCKY YOUR INSANITY?
SHH!!
O-OKAY!
THAT'S SOLICITATION. LET'S BRING HER IN!

IT'S GOING TO GET TIGHT IN THERE. YOU READY?
RIGHT BEHIND YOU.
OKAY THEN.

YOU THERE! FREEZE!
GABBLE?
STAY RIGHT THERE, MISS. YOU'RE UNDER ARREST.

GABBLE!!
DAMN IT!
COME BACK HERE!

COME ON, JEONG!!
RIGHT BEHIND YOU!
GABBLE!

NIKKO
ビール

EEP
VNN

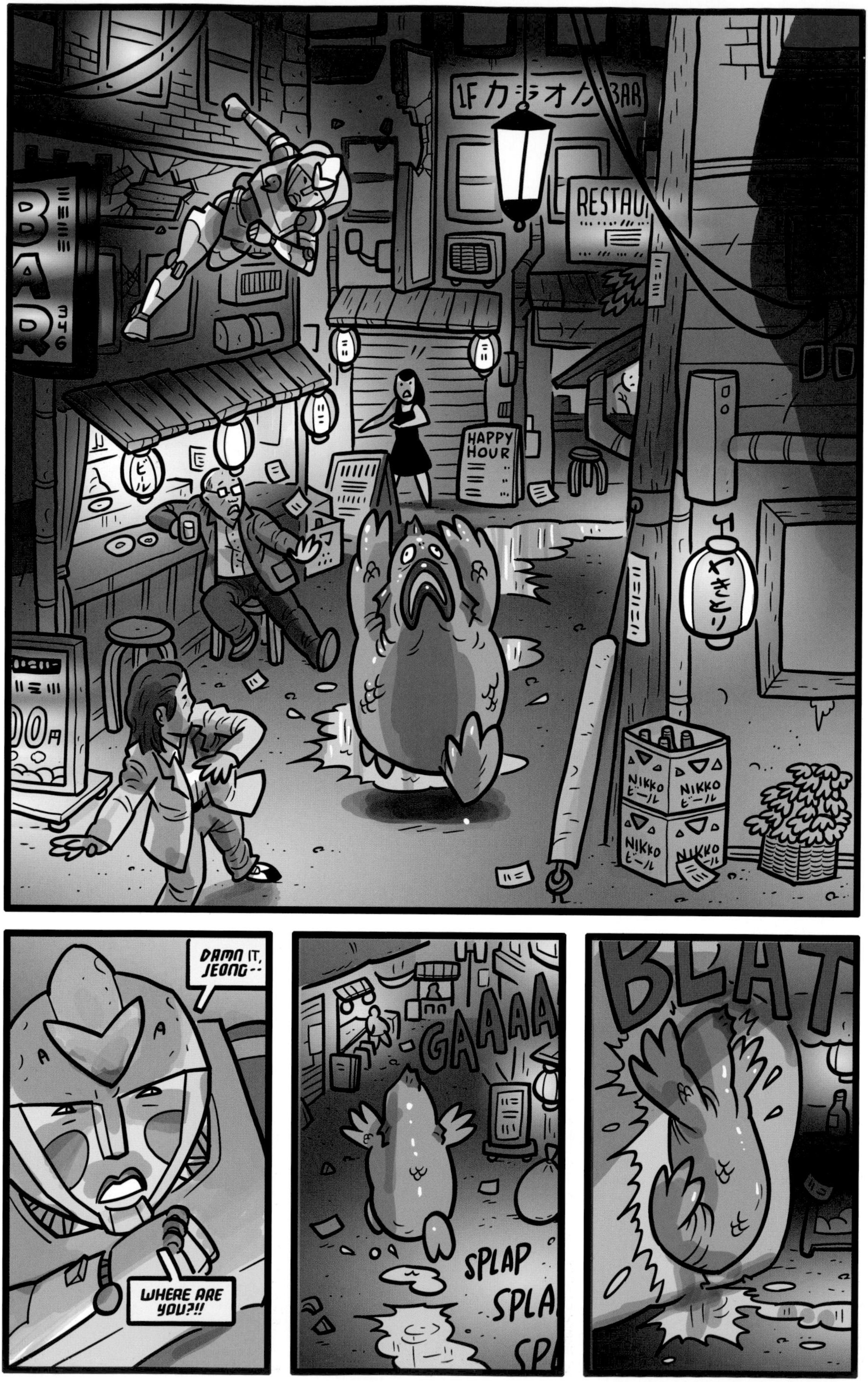

1F カラオケ BAR
RESTAU
BAR
HAPPY HOUR
ビール
NIKKO ビール
やきとり

DAMN IT, JEONG--
WHERE ARE YOU?!!

GAAAA
SPLAP
SPLA
SP

BLAT

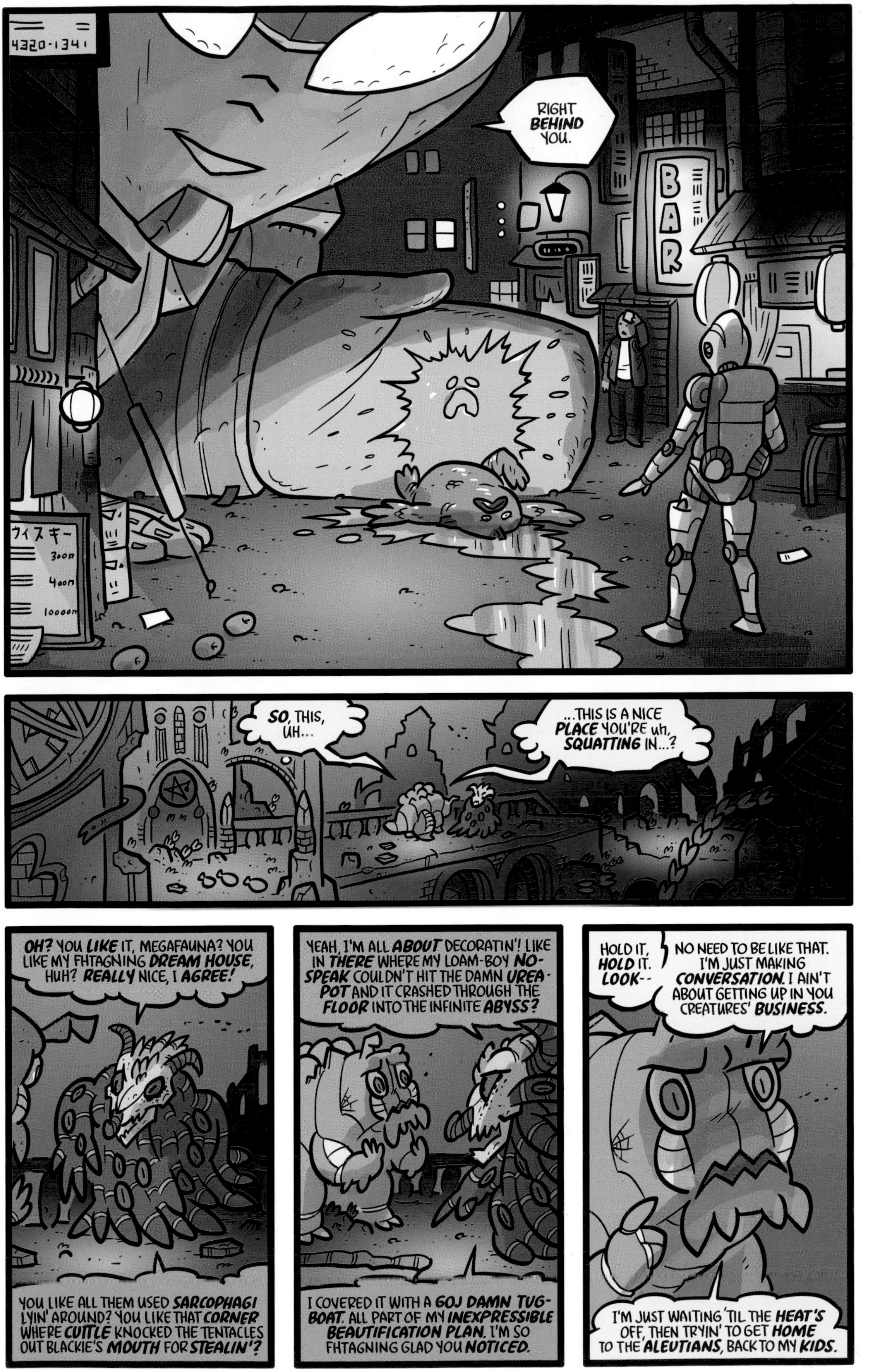

4320-1341

RIGHT BEHIND YOU.

BAR

ウィスキー
300円
400円
10000円

"YOU CREATURES."
FHTAGN YOU.

WE THE SAME CREATURES. YOU AIN'T BETTER.
YOU KNOW ANY MON UP THERE HAVE ONE BAD AEON, AND HE DOWN HERE WITH US.
ALL LYIN' HERE, SAYIN' YOU'LL KICK WHEN THE STARS ARE RIGHT...

BUT SHEEEEEOL, LIZZA...
THE STARS AIN'T NEVER RIGHT.
CALLING ME

GOAT

SO YOU GOT KIDS, HUH? BIG BAD BOYS, WRECKIN' AMBERGRIS UP, I BET?
BOY AND A GIRL. AND NAH, THEY'RE BOTH GOOD KIDS.

OH FHTAGN NO. A GIRL, TOO? HA! YOU GONNA WISH YOU JUST HAD BOYS. SHE GONNA BE ALL SLITHERIN' OUT, GETTIN' KNOCKED UP, ALL GETTIN' MIXED UP WITH CULTS YOU DON'T KNOW...
YO, THE STUFF I DID? SHE GONNA RUN YOU RAGGED, DAD.

IT AIN'T LIKE THAT. SHE'S A GOOD GIRL.
OH? YOU KEEPIN' A CLOSE EYE ON HER?
MY MOMS SHOWED ME THE BACK OF HER TENTACLE NONSTOP FOR STRANGE AEONS, YO, AND LOOK AT ME NOW.
GETTIN' CRAZY IN A KRAKEN HOUSE...

BUT YO, I AIN'T HATIN', THOUGH. SHE COOL.
IT WAS JUST THAT THAT BOYFRIEND OF HERS...
A-ANYWAY THAT'S ALL ANCIENT HISTORY UP IN SPACE.

SO LIKE, I COME DOWN, TRY TO GET STRAIGHT.
CLEAN UP NICE, GET A CULT GOIN' GET THAT WEEKLY SACRIFICE, THAT KA-CHING, YOU KNOW?
FIND A HOUSE, BECAUSE YOU KNOW NO MATTER WHAT ELSE A GIRL GOT TO DO...

...SHE GOT TO TAKE CARE OF HER BABIES.
IÄÄÄ!!
IÄÄÄ
OH MY GOJ.

HEY! SHUT UP DOWN THERE! I'M FHTAGNING BUSY. YOU GOT FHTAGNING FOOD-- EAT IT AND ABSORB ITS POWER, STUPID!
UH...
IÄÄÄÄÄ

...THESE ARE ALL YOUR KIDS?
WHO ARE THEIR DADS?
THAT'S HOW A GIRL'S LIFE BE, YOU HEARD?
EVERYONE HIT.
SOMETIMES YOU GOT TO STICK CLOSE TO AN O.G., YOU WANNA BE SAFE.
SOMETIMES, WELL, THAT'S JUST WHAT THE CRATES COST. CUTTLE AIN'T GIVIN' NOTHIN' AWAY FREE.

THAT'S JUST HOW IT IS, AN' HOW IT'S ALWAYS GONNA BE.
PAST, PRESENT, AND FUTURE ARE ALL ONE, KNOW WHAT I'M SAYIN'?

YOUR GIRL GONNA FIND OUT. SHE BE PLAYIN' NOW, BUT SHE GONNA WANT TO FIND A MON WHO CAN GET HER WHAT SHE NEED.

YOU KNOW, ONCE YOU AIN'T AROUND TO PROTECT HER NO MORE.

INTERVIEW THREE

JEONG?
YOU OUT HERE?
NOTI

HEY. I GOT HER ALL SET TO GO. WAIVED THE LAWYER AND EVERY-THING. YOU READY?
YEAH.
BE IN IN JUST A SEC.

FFP

SHING

HHUH

JEONG. Hey. Over HERE. Interview THREE.

You all RIGHT?
YEAH. Yeah, all SET. WHOO
SO. You DONE an interview before?
You know how this WORKS?

The ACADEMY didn't really have much for me to DOWNLOAD, but it's just asking QUESTIONS, right?
Not REALLY. Nobody gives up NOTHIN' on their OWN.
But you give THEM a story where they're the HERO, or failing THAT, the VICTIM, they'll fill in ALL the blanks for you.
Something BIG. Bigger than THEM.

Made it so they HAD to do what they did.
It's not their FAULT.
It's PATHETIC, but they go for it every TIME.

OKAY THEN, MISS HAVERSHAM...

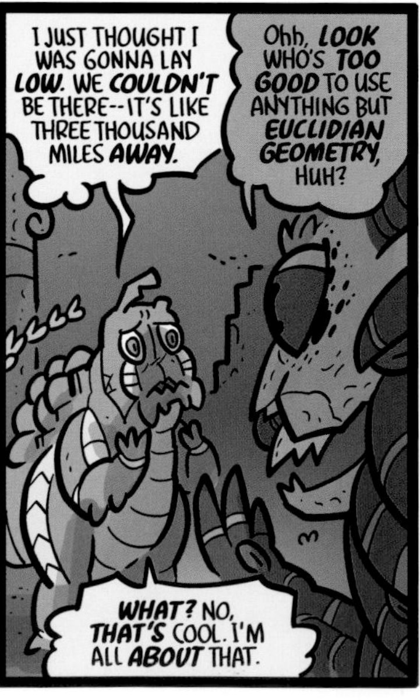

WHO THE **FHTAGN** IS **DIS?**

...!

Y-YEAH, YOU KNOW, A LI'L TASTE WOULD BE GOOD, CUTTLE...
I KNOW IT WOULD. I KNOW YOU LIKE THE CRAZY.
I EVEN GOT SOME FORBIDDEN ARTIFACTS TO SMOOTH OUT THAT RIDE. I KNOW YOU LIKE THAT.

YEAH. YEAH. J-JUST LEMME--
OW!
YO, 'CEPT WHO'S THIS OFF-BRAND MEGAFAUNA YOU GOT TAKIN' UP SPACE IN HERE?
FTAGN LIFE
YEAH, YOU. WHERE THE FHTAGN YOU FROM?

JUST PASSIN' THROUGH, MY LIZZA. I DON'T MEAN TO--
DON'T MEAN TO WHAT? MOVE IN ON MY SHUB WHILE I'M OUT EARNIN'?
EAT MY FOOD? BREATHE MY WATER?
BE DREAMIN' UP IN MY HOUSE WHILE I'M OUT DOIN' THE NECESSARY?
FHTAGN NO, "MY LIZZA."

Y-YO, WHAT YOU SAYIN', "MY HOUSE?" YOU KNOW THIS IS MY HOUSE, CUTTLE. Y-YOU JUST CRASHING HERE.
SHUB, IT WAS YOUR HOUSE, BUT YOU COULDN'T PAY, SO I BROUGHT MY LOAMIES AND OUR BUSINESS IN, AN' NOW IT'S OUR HOUSE.
MY HOUSE.

Y-YEAH, YOU SAID YOU WAS GONNA PAY ME, CUTTLE, SO YOUR BOYS COULD COME GET CRAZY. BUT I AIN'T BEEN PAID IN STRANGE AEONS, YO.
Y-YOU JUST TALK FAST, A-AN' KEEP ME DOPED ON THE MYSTERIES. THAT AIN'T RIGHT.
TH-THAT AIN'T RIGHT.
F-FHTAGN. YOU THINK YOU THE BOSS, BUT YOU AIN'T EVEN. WE ALL BEEN IN THE GAME AS LONG AS YOU, OR LONGER.
YOU WEAK. JUST EVERY-ONE KNOWS YOUR NAME IS ALL.

SMOK

SEE, I DON'T EVEN WANT TO DO THAT. THAT WHAT I'M ABOUT, YOU KNOW?
NNG
BUT YOU WANT TO PUSH AGAINST MY AUTHORITY, THAT KIND OF AMBERGRIS START TO HAPPEN.

LIKE WHEN YOU FIRST COME TO ME, WHEN YOUR MOMS KICKED YOU OUT OF SPACE. I LET YOU BE MY SHUB. GAVE YOU A TASTE. BUT YOU LEFT, GOAT.
LEFT ME.
ALL YOU DUNWICHES THE SAME. YOU NEED SOMEONE TO PROTECT YOU, YOU KNOW WHAT THAT COST. YOU THINK YOU TOO GOOD FOR THAT? YOU AIN'T.

YOU STILL THE SAME STUPID KRAKEN-HEAD THAT'LL DO ANYTHING FOR A HIT, AND CAN'T DO NOTHIN' ON HER OWN.
SH-SHUT UP, CUTTLE...
YEAH?
THAT WHAT YOU WANT TO SAY TO ME? I WILL--
...!
THAP

WH--?

D-DID **YOU** JUST--
S-STOP!!
WHAT--
WHAT ARE YOU **DOING?!!**

WHOOM
STOP!!

PLEASE--

GET THE FHTAGN **OFF** HIM, MEGAFAUNA! WHAT THE FHTAGN IS **WRONG** WITH YOU?!
WE GOT A FHTAGNING **SYSTEM**. YOU DON'T JUST COME IN HERE AN' **WRECK** THAT.
YOU **HEAR** ME? THIS HOW WE **LIVE**, MEGAFAUNA!!

HUHH
THAT AIN'T HOW LIFE SHOULD BE.
YOU AIN'T BEEN TREATED RIGHT. IT'S MADE YOU SOMETHING ELSE.
YOU NEED TO GET OUT.
TALK TO SOMEONE.
SOMEONE WHO CAN HELP YOU.

SNIFF
WELL, AIN'T YOU SMART. AIN'T YOU GOOD.
WH-WHY DON'T YOU TELL ME, THEN...

WHO?
"SO.
"You two learn anything NEW?"

Sure DID, Colonel. Where she's FROM, there's a whole OPERATION going. DRUGS, PROSTITUTION, some kinds of DEALS to improve the FISHING in the BAY...
Also, TIME'S a FLAT CIRCLE, but I don't know how that fits IN.
Not much we can PROVE or send to the D.A., unfortunately.
But what's really USEFUL isn't what she's SEEN down there...

...it's what she's seeing NOW.
We found your FUGITIVE.
You did WHAT?!
YEAH.
Turns out they got this GROUP MIND. It syncs UP when they're all LIVING together.

Wh-- The TEAM G.R.E.A.T. SATELLITE has MAPPED that whole HOUSING PROJECT down there and it's seen no SIGN of him.
Well, something DOWN THERE has.
You want to throw the COORDINATES on there, Chisato?

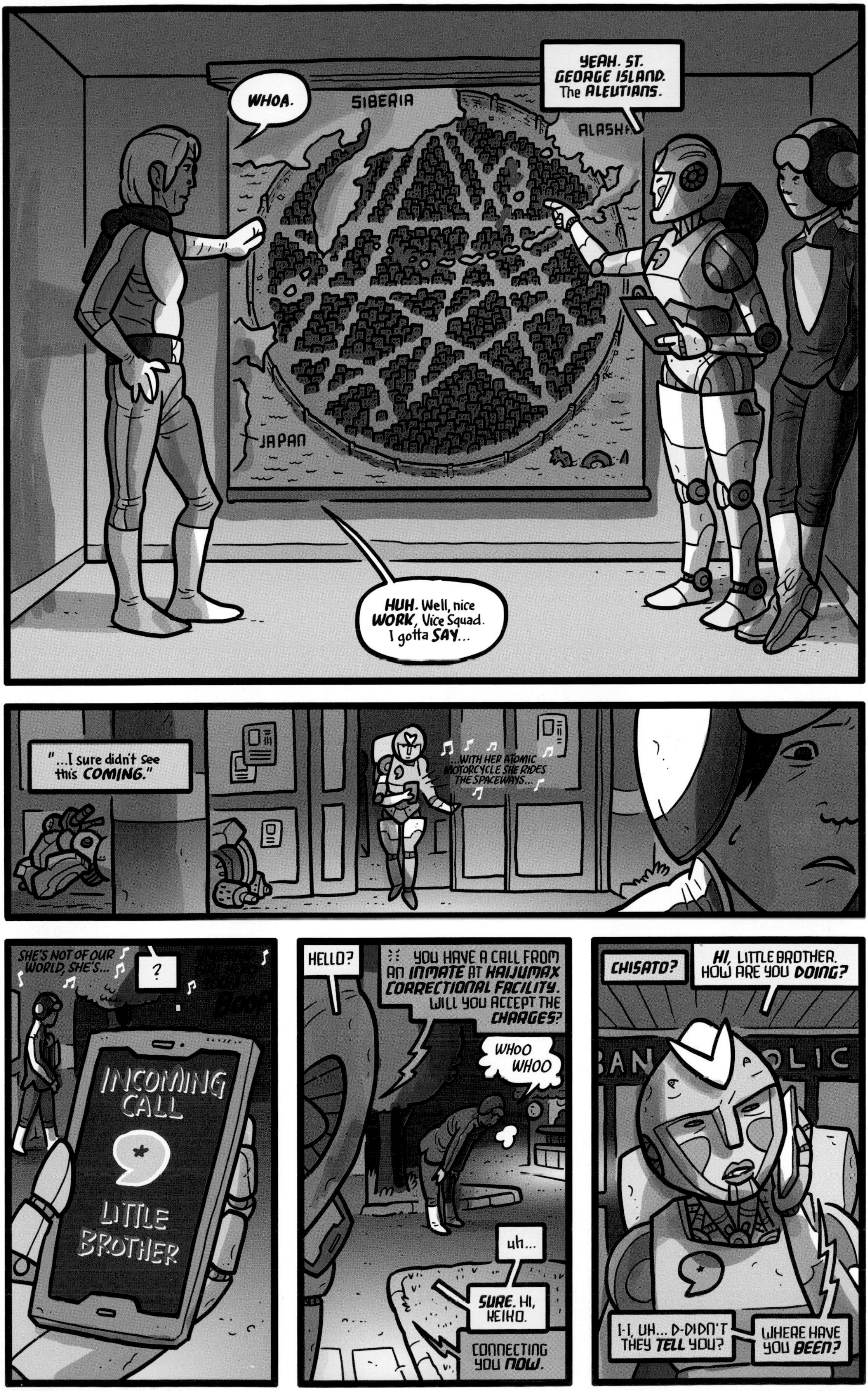

WHOA.
SIBERIA
ALASKA
JAPAN
YEAH. ST. GEORGE ISLAND. The ALEUTIANS.
HUH. Well, nice WORK, Vice Squad. I gotta SAY...

"...I sure didn't see this COMING."
...WITH HER ATOMIC MOTORCYCLE SHE RIDES THE SPACEWAYS...

SHE'S NOT OF OUR WORLD, SHE'S...
?
INCOMING CALL
LITTLE BROTHER

HELLO?
YOU HAVE A CALL FROM AN INMATE AT KAIJUMAX CORRECTIONAL FACILITY. WILL YOU ACCEPT THE CHARGES?
WHOO WHOO
uh...
SURE. HI, KEIKO.
CONNECTING YOU NOW.

CHISATO?
HI, LITTLE BROTHER. HOW ARE YOU DOING?
I-I, UH... D-DIDN'T THEY TELL YOU?
WHERE HAVE YOU BEEN?

"I'M **SORRY.** NOBODY SAW IT **COMING.**

"HE'S **GONE.**"

EPISODE 5

怪獣マックス

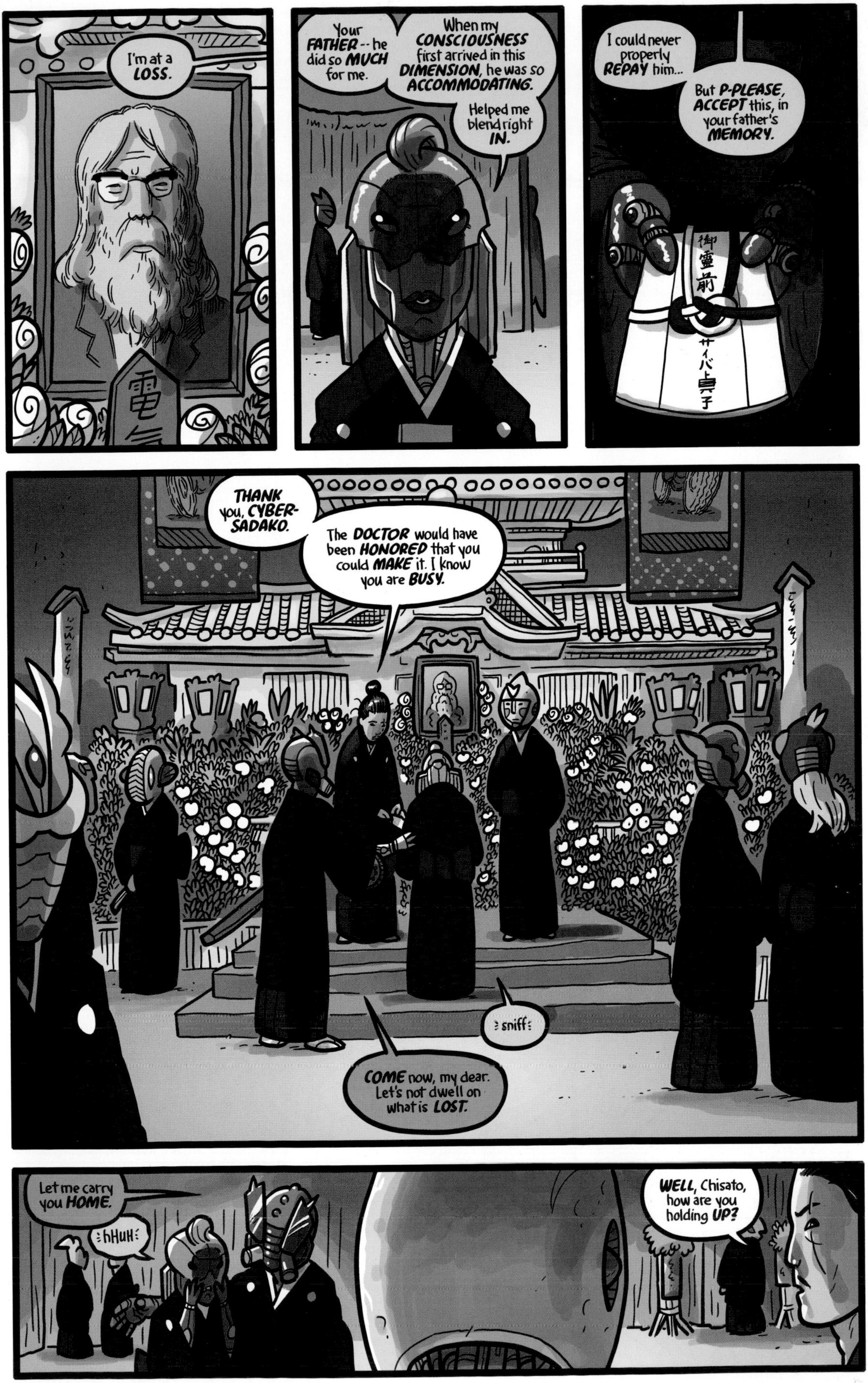

I'm at a **LOSS.**

Your **FATHER** -- he did so **MUCH** for me.
When my **CONSCIOUSNESS** first arrived in this **DIMENSION**, he was so **ACCOMMODATING.**
Helped me blend right **IN.**

I could never properly **REPAY** him...
But **P-PLEASE, ACCEPT** this, in your father's **MEMORY.**
御霊前
サイバー貞子

THANK you, **CYBER-SADAKO.**
The **DOCTOR** would have been **HONORED** that you could **MAKE** it. I know you are **BUSY.**
sniff
COME now, my dear. Let's not dwell on what is **LOST.**

Let me carry you **HOME.**
hHuH
WELL, Chisato, how are you holding **UP?**

All right, I guess. It's just so SUDDEN, a HEART ATTACK.
Oh, REALLY?

I guess I feel like he was DECLINING for quite some TIME. The COUGHING, and all. It's been MONTHS.
THERE we go.
But you know your FATHER. STUBBORN. Not one to be told what to DO, what MEDICINE to take.

YEAH. I know he never missed your afternoon TEA, no matter WHAT anyone else was doing.
HA! Isn't THAT the truth!
He'd have me in the DIAGNOSTIC CAR of the DRILL TRAIN for an HOUR while you and he did the whole CEREMONY.

Well, that was a special TIME that we had. Lot of FUTURE PLANS discussed. I think of them FONDLY now he's GONE.
I think he must have KNOWN his time was SHORT.

The way he CONFIDED in me.
ANYWAY, Chisato, you can be CERTAIN that DENKI ROBOTICS will CONTINUE under my watch.
There's nothing to WORRY about. I've got it all under CONTROL.

OKAY then. I can take that OFFERING the SWORD-WOMAN gave you and sort things OUT with the FUNERAL HOME.
No NEED, no NEED.
I made sure DENKI did a lot of BUSINESS with them PRO-BONO, so this is on the HOUSE.

But--
These OFFERINGS will offset the temporary HIT our lab will TAKE in the wake of your father's DEATH. Just until we get on our FEET again.
Ah.
There's my NINE O'CLOCK MEETING.

You don't worry about a THING. Your father would have WANTED you to FOCUS on your WORK.
I've got it ALL under CONTROL.

Gentle beings of the COUNCIL!
How was your JOURNEY from the NEBULA of the ETERNAL SUNRISE?
VERY GOOD, THANK YOU.
Shall we go SIT DOWN in the next ROOM?

YES, WELL, WE HAD HOPED TO SEE A DEMONSTRATION OF THE DRONES YOU SUGGESTED.
All in good TIME, all in good time.
May I offer you some COFFEE?

LITTLE SISTER. ARE YOU WELL? DO YOU NEED TO TALK OR GRIEVE?
BY NOW YOU MUST BE IN STAGE TWO OF--

NO.
EVERYTHING'S FINE, HEARSE-O-TRON 3000.
I'M HANDLING IT.
I'M DOING EXACTLY WHAT I'M SUPPOSED TO.

NOW, IF YOU'LL **EXCUSE** ME...

FRIENDS ON THE OUTSIDE

WELL, YOUR BROTHER'S A CRIMINAL ON FURLOUGH, PARTNER.
I CAN'T POWER DOWN AND LEAVE HIM UNATTENDED.
I MEAN, I--

FINE.
FINE.
YOU GO AHEAD AND STAY BIG AND ARMORED UP UNTIL YOU RUST.
I'LL GO BACK AND FIGURE OUT WHAT OTHER CRAP GORO'S GOTTEN US INTO.
SISTER, PLEASE--

SIGH
WHAT.
THERE IS A TIME FOR ALL THINGS. OBSOLESCENCE COMES FOR US ALL.
THE CLOUD SHOWS US THAT EVEN IN ADVERSITY, WE CAN FIND A SMALL AMOUNT OF PEACE IN--

YEAH. YEAH, I GET IT. IF THERE'S AN OHM DROPPED IN THE DATASTREAM, I JUST FLOW AROUND IT. I'VE HEARD IT ALL BEFORE.
IT'S ALL EASY FOR YOU, WHEN YOU NEVER EVEN LIKED DAD.

YEAH. I KNOW. HE WAS MEAN TO YOU. BIG DEAL.
BUT YOU COULD DO IT FOR ME.
CHISATO, YOU KNOW I WOULD DO ANYTHING FOR--
FORGET IT.
I GOTTA GET BACK.

I'LL BE OUT IN A MINUTE.
AND THEN WE CAN TAKE YOU BACK TO PRISON.

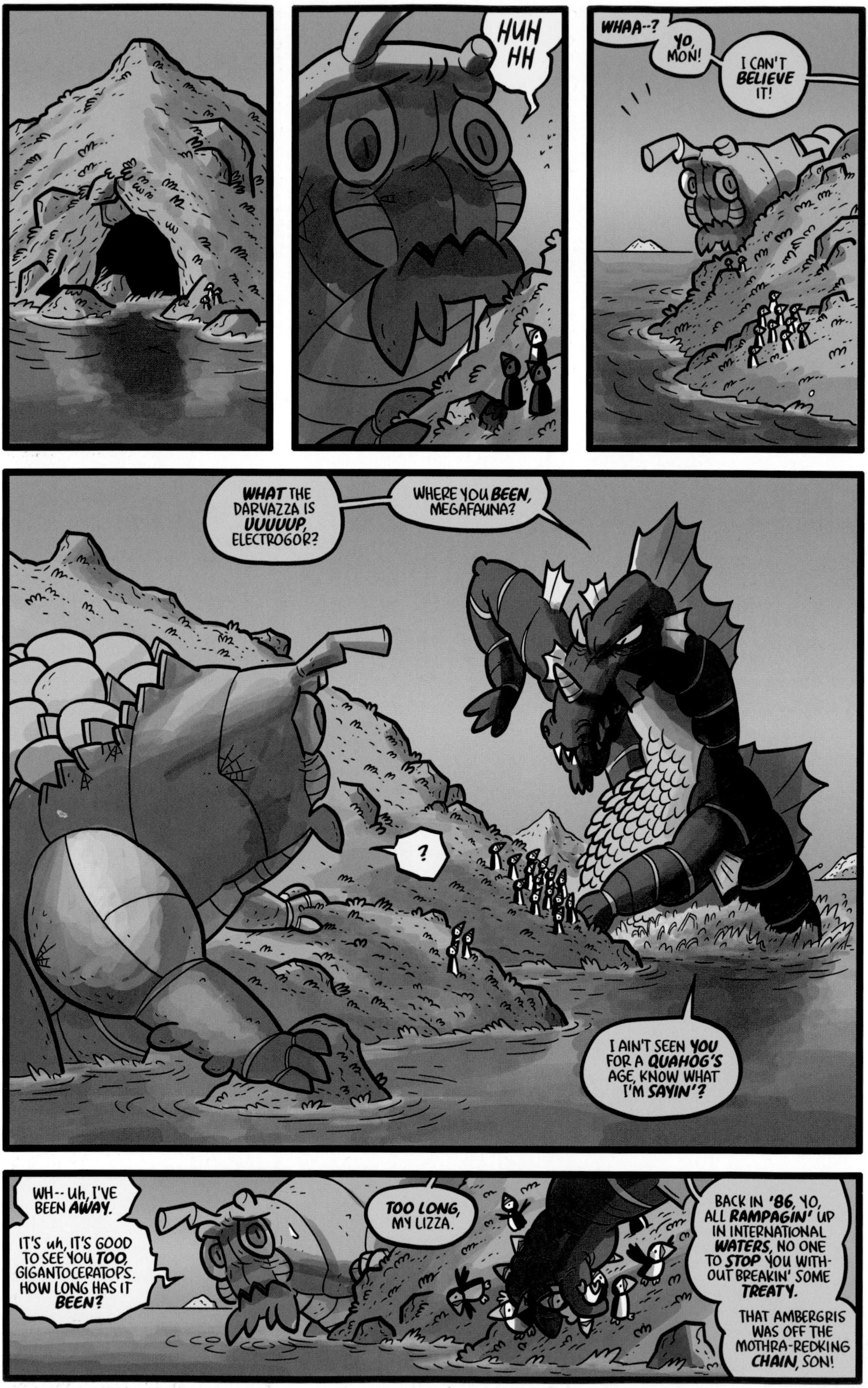

WHAT THE DARVAZZA IS **UUUUUP**, ELECTROGOR?

WHERE YOU **BEEN**, MEGAFAUNA?

?

I AIN'T SEEN **YOU** FOR A **QUAHOG'S** AGE, KNOW WHAT I'M **SAYIN'**?

SO WHAT ARE YOU DOING DOWN HERE, MON? ALL OUTSIDE THE SHIPPING LANES?
AIN'T MUCH HAPPENING AROUND THESE PARTS.
CROMF

WELL, I JUST GOT HERE. I BEEN DODGING THE COPS AND I-I'M CATCHING MY BREATH.
I-IT'S JUST THAT I HAVEN'T BEEN BACK IN SO LONG, I-I'M SCARED WHAT I MIGHT FIND.

OH, IN THERE? MARIANAS NO, MY LIZZA, YOU JUST GOT TO JUMP IN.
SHE GOT IT ALL READY FOR YOU. I'LL WAIT. YOU GO AHEAD.

"SHE?"
YEAH, YOU DON'T GOT TO TALK TO THE OTHER ONE.
LIZZA, WHERE YOU BEEN? AIN'T YOU NEVER COME HERE BEFORE?

I'VE BEEN IN PRISON. K-MAX. DOWN SOUTH.
AND YEAH, I'VE BEEN HERE BEFORE. I LIVE HERE. I'VE NEARLY KILLED MYSELF GETTING HERE.
WHO ARE YOU TALKING ABOUT?

Uhh...
Y-YO, MY LIZZA...
I'M JUST GONNA...
LIKE...
I GOTTA GO.

FLAP FLAP FLAP

"HERE WE ARE. HOME SWEET HOME."

INTAKE

INTAKE

YES, I SUPPOSE IT **IS**.

:sigh:
ALL RIGHT, YOU SET?
YES, MY SISTER.
ARE YOU SET?
ARE YOUR CHIPS SET IN THEIR PROPER SOCKETS? IN THE WAKE OF A BIG CHANGE IT'S IMPORTANT TO UPDATE OUR DRIVERS AND--

OOKAY. SO I GUESS I'LL SEE YOU LATER.
AKE
SISTER, PLEASE.
I KNOW YOU'RE UPSET WITH ME CAN'T WE TALK?

TALK? TO YOU? WHY? YOU DON'T CARE.
EVERYTHING'S JUST A PHILOSOPHICAL ARGUMENT TO YOU.
YOU DON'T CARE ABOUT REAL-LIFE PROBLEMS IN THE FACE OF ALL YOUR BIG IDEAS.
INTAKE
I-I MEAN...
WH-WHAT IF I TOLD YOU I THINK GORO KILLED DAD, MECHAZON? HUH?

OH, SISTER, IT WAS A HEART ATTACK. DAD'S BEEN GETTING SICKER AND SICKER FOR MONTHS. WE SAW IT.
SICKER BECAUSE GORO'S BEEN MAKING HIM SICKER!
THE--THE TEA HE'S ALWAYS GIVING HIM. IT'S "GOT TO BE PREPARED A CERTAIN WAY." A-ALL HIS PLANS HE'S GOT. HE NEEDED DAD DEAD TO DO THEM.

DON'T YOU SEE IT? HE'S A LIAR. A LIAR!
:sniff:
HEART ATTACK, MY SHINY METAL ASS!
YOU PROBABLY DON'T BELIEVE ME. I DON'T CARE. IT PROBABLY DOES SOUND CRAZY.
BUT IT'S TRUE. AND YOU KNOW IT IS. AND I'M GOING TO DO SOMETHING ABOUT IT.

SISTER...
LET GO OF ME.
THAT MEATBAG NEEDS TO DIE.
CHISATO...! WHAT ARE YOU--
HE KILLED DAD. RIGHT IN FRONT OF OUR EYES. FOR YEARS. ALL FOR A WEAPONS CONTRACT.
I'M GOING TO KILL HIM, AND HE'S GOING TO KNOW EXACTLY WHY.

CHI-CHAN, PLEASE. PLEASE. YOU MUSTN'T.
VIOLENCE IS NOT THE WAY. THE CLOUD TELLS US TO FORGIVE THOSE WHO HAVE DAMAGED US.
NOT FOR THEIR SAKES, BUT FOR OURS.
NOTHING IS MORE VALUABLE TO THE CLOUD THAN A LIFE LIVED IN CONTENTMENT.

WHAT A BUNCH OF--
SISTER, I HAVE SPENT MOST OF MY LIFE TRYING TO DISENGAGE FROM THE DESIRES OF THE CORRUPT MEAT WORLD.
TO MEDITATE IN THE CLOUD, TO BE BEYOND THE CARES OF THE WORLD, THAT IS A PEACE LIKE NOTHING YOU HAVE EVER EXPERIENCED.

YOU KEEP LIVING HERE, THEN. CUT ALL YOUR TIES. GIVE UP ALL YOUR FRIENDS ON THE OUTSIDE.
AND THEN TAKE YOUR CLOUD AND SHOVE IT UP YOUR EXHAUST PIPE.

SKRRKK
COME IN, OFFICER DENKI, OFFICER JEONG.
YEAH, JEONG HERE.
JEONG, THIS IS DISPATCH.
WE GOT A REASSIGNMENT FOR YOU. YOU'RE TO HEAD UP TO ANCHORAGE, ALASKA. WE GOT A CALL IN THAT'S BEEN BOUNCED TO VICE.

SAY AGAIN, DISPATCH. YOU'RE CALLING US TO A VICE BUST IN ALASKA?
THAT'S WHAT MY COMPUTER SAYS-- SEEMS LIKE THERE ARE OTHERS WHO COULD DO IT, BUT YOU'RE UP.
ALL RIGHT, THEN. ALTERING COURSE FOR ALASKA. JEONG OUT.

OKAY, YOU HEAR THAT, PARTNER? I GUESS WE'RE NOT GOING BACK TO NAGOYA AFTER ALL. WE--
HEY, YOU ALL RIGHT?
UNBELIEVABLE.

IT'S MY X#8%ING BROTHER. I SAID SOMETHING TO HIM THAT--
WELL, ANYWAY. HE DID THIS. HE SAYS HE DOESN'T HAVE ANY FRIENDS ON THE OUTSIDE, BUT HE MADE THIS HAPPEN.

IT'S MY OWN GOJ-DAMN LIFE. I CAN GO BACK TO NAGOYA IF I WANT. HIM AND HIS EMPTY SELF-RIGHTEOUS PROVERBS, THEY'RE JUST--
EVERYTHING, GOJ-DAMN EVERYTHING, MAKING ME JUST--

KDOOM

CHISATO!!

I'M OKAY, I'M OKAY. NNNGH
OWWW.

JUST-- BLEW A STUPID FUSE. NNG I'M JUST--
HEY, HEY, SHH. SIT STILL. LET ME TAKE A LOOK AT IT.

HOLD ON, YEAH. I SEE IT.
OWW-- NNF S-STUPID BODY. STUPID--
SNIFF

S-STUPID GOJ-DAMN EVERYTHING--
G-GORO KILLED MY DAD, AND MY B-BROTHER AND HIS STUPID RELIGION--
HHUHH
HEY. HEY. YOU'RE OKAY. LET IT OUT.

I CAN ALMOST GET THE... VALVE WITH MY FINGERS HERE.
JUST A LITTLE NARROW. JUST--
Aah, FORGET IT.
SHING

HOLD ON. I GOTTA GET IN THERE.

WHOO WHOO
OKAY.
YOU ALL RIGHT UP THERE?
Yeah. YEAH. I'm OKAY. I GOT this.

HNNG
HHNG!!
ALMOST...
HHHNG

HHUH
HHUH
KEEK
YOU GOT IT?

Yeah. YEAH. GOT it.
HUHH
P-please get me DOWN.
JEONG? YOU OKAY?

Yeah, I--
HUHH
I'm gonna get SQUISHED
HUHH
I'm gonna get SQUISHED
I'm
SHING

HHUH
GONNA GET SQUISHED

HEY.
HEY.
YOU'RE OKAY. EVERYTHING'S OKAY. YOU'RE SAFE.
I-I JUST CAN'T--
HHUH HUH
I-I'M JUST--

YOU'RE OKAY. YOU HAVE TO BE OKAY.
YOU HAVE TO. PLEASE.
HUHH
PLEASE, JIN-WOOK.
PLEASE.

YOU'RE THE ONLY GOOD THING IN MY LIFE.

YOU'RE--
YOU'RE THE ONLY GOOD THING IN MY LIFE, TOO.

VOGO?
TORGAX?
HELLO?

K-KIDS? ARE YOU HERE?
A-ARE YOU--
!

OH, GOJ--

HHUH

WHAT--

HHUH
Oh MY GOJ.

VOGO!!
TORGAX!!
ANSWER ME!!

"DAD, YOU'RE BACK!"

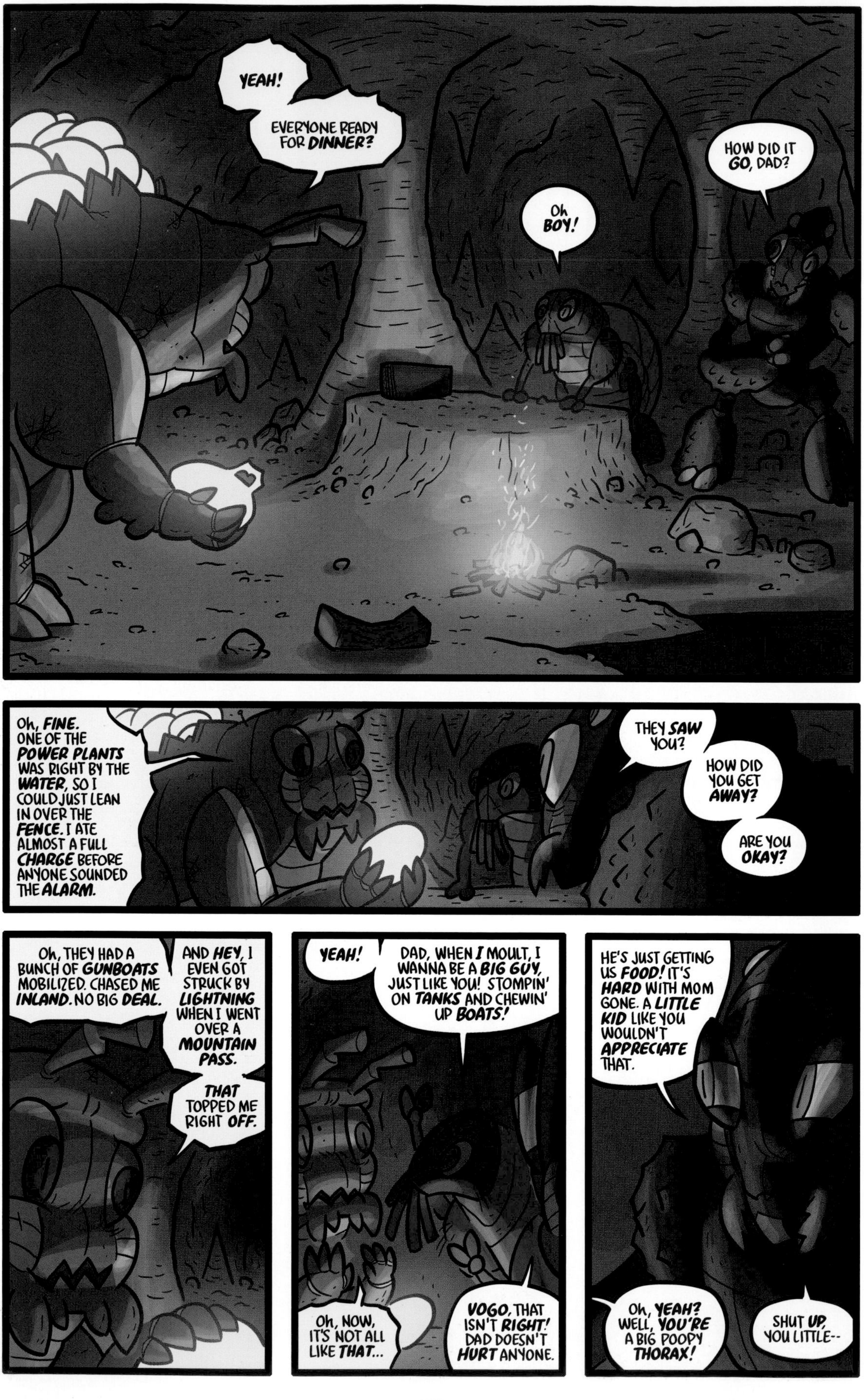

YEAH!
EVERYONE READY FOR DINNER?
Oh BOY!
HOW DID IT GO, DAD?

Oh, FINE. ONE OF THE POWER PLANTS WAS RIGHT BY THE WATER, SO I COULD JUST LEAN IN OVER THE FENCE. I ATE ALMOST A FULL CHARGE BEFORE ANYONE SOUNDED THE ALARM.
THEY SAW YOU?
HOW DID YOU GET AWAY?
ARE YOU OKAY?

Oh, THEY HAD A BUNCH OF GUNBOATS MOBILIZED. CHASED ME INLAND. NO BIG DEAL.
AND HEY, I EVEN GOT STRUCK BY LIGHTNING WHEN I WENT OVER A MOUNTAIN PASS.
THAT TOPPED ME RIGHT OFF.

YEAH!
DAD, WHEN I MOULT, I WANNA BE A BIG GUY, JUST LIKE YOU! STOMPIN' ON TANKS AND CHEWIN' UP BOATS!
Oh, NOW, IT'S NOT ALL LIKE THAT...
VOGO, THAT ISN'T RIGHT! DAD DOESN'T HURT ANYONE.

HE'S JUST GETTING US FOOD! IT'S HARD WITH MOM GONE. A LITTLE KID LIKE YOU WOULDN'T APPRECIATE THAT.
Oh, YEAH? WELL, YOU'RE A BIG POOPY THORAX!
SHUT UP, YOU LITTLE--

KIDS, KIDS!
COME ON, DON'T BATTLE.
I'M BACK. WE'VE GOT ENOUGH TO EAT. AND I'VE GOT YOU TWO.

NOW LET'S HAVE A NICE DINNER, HUH?

KIDS, PLEASE...

sniff

?
SKTCH

HEY--
HEY, WHO'S--

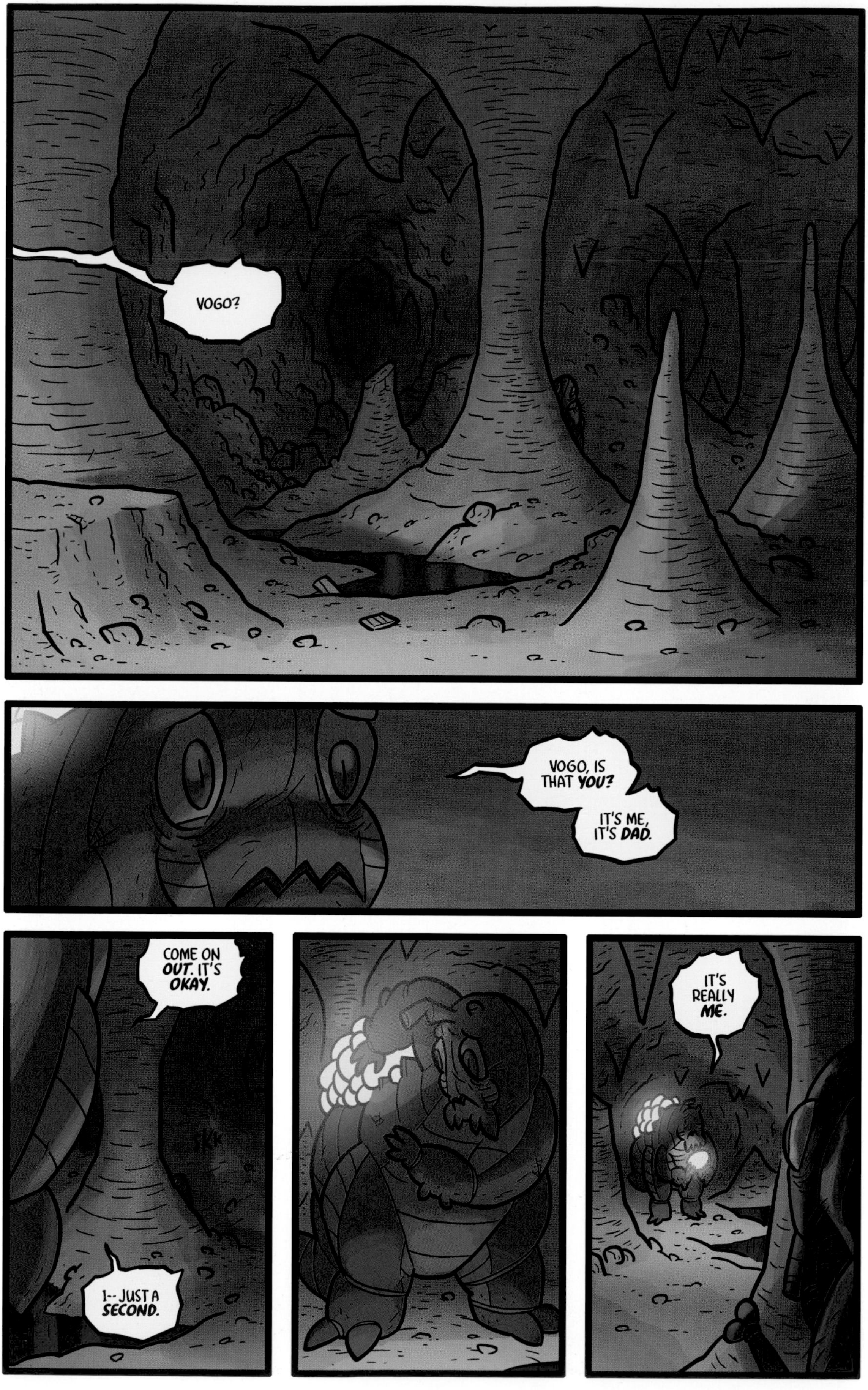

VOGO?

VOGO, IS THAT YOU?
IT'S ME, IT'S DAD.

COME ON OUT. IT'S OKAY.
I-- JUST A SECOND.

IT'S REALLY ME.

Oh, MY **BOY**.

Oh, MY BABY **BOY**.

"I FOUND YOU."

COMPUTER, switch ON.
AUTHORI-ZATION code 16420. GORO.

Initiate DRONE ATTACK sequence 63: CLOUD OF HELL. Weapons on SAFETY.
We're going to need to show the council something SPECIAL if we want this CONTRACT, my little friends.

DING
BLOCKED
TOASTER CAM
What the--

Computer, OVERRIDE.
The DOCTOR is GONE. I'M the administrator now.
DZZT
COMPUTER...

OVERRIDE. 16420. It's ME. GORO.
TKTAK
I'm STANDING right HERE.

And what's with changing the damn WALLPAPER? Who even put the DOC'S face on my--
DZZT

...terminal...
BLAM

Wh--
Who--

DZZT
Who-.
HHKHKKK~

DZZT

DZZT
H.E.R.O.I.S.M. HQ.

DZZT
ADMIN, ARE YOU FEELING ALL RIGHT?

DZZT
...A BIT OF PEACEFUL **MEDITATION** IS ALL THAT'S **REQUIRED**.

EPISODE 6

怪獣マックス

WHOOFY™

DAD, WE CAN WAIT FOR TORGAX TO COME BACK...
NO. WE HAVE TO GO GET HER. I NEED TO GET US ALL TOGETHER AND WE NEED TO GET OUT OF HERE.

I'VE GOT A PLAN. WE CAN HEAD SOUTH, UNDERWATER TO STAY OFF THE GRID.
GET TO LAKE MARACAIBO. STORM CENTRAL. LOTS OF FOOD THERE.
THIS PLACE, IT'S NOT SAFE ANYMORE.
TORGAX MAKES IT SAFE, DAD. AND WITH THE TWO OF YOU--

NO. TORGAX IS STILL IN HER NYMPH STAGE. I THINK IT'S GREAT THAT SHE'S STOMPED UP AND HAS BEEN GOING OUT ON HER OWN TO GET FOOD FOR YOU TWO, BUT I'M HERE NOW.
I GOT THIS UNDER CONTROL. BUT WE GOTTA GET HER, AND WE GOTTA GET OUT OF HERE.

TORGAX SAID WE CAN'T GO, DAD. SHE--
VOGO, I KNOW. SHE WAS RIGHT. BUT THAT WAS SO I COULD FIND YOU HERE, AND I'M BACK NOW.
BUT--
NO, DAD, SHE SAID SHE'S GOT CLIENTS THAT NEED TO KNOW WHERE TO FIND HER. SHE'S GOT TO MAKE MONEY.

SHE'S... WHAT?

"Uh... HER BODY, IT CHANGED, DAD, AND SHE LOOKS DIFFERENT NOW."
"SHE SAID THAT NOW MONS WOULD PAY HER TO LET THEM LICK URANIUM OFF HER SHELL."

SH-SHE WHAT?
SHE SAID IT'S NO BIG DEAL, DAD.
IT'S JUST MONEY.

I-IT--
W-WELL, NONE OF THAT STUFF MATTERS. WE GOT OUR THINGS. LET'S GO.
I'M GOING TO FIND MY LITTLE GIRL, AND THEN WE'RE ALL LEAVING.

OKAY, BUT I MEAN, I WANT YOU TO KNOW, DAD...

...SHE'S NOT THAT *LITTLE* ANYMORE.

ABOVE 9000

FREEZE! ALL RIGHT, YOU. HOLD IT RIGHT THERE.
YOU GOT HER, CHISATO?
IN MY SIGHTS.
MISS, YOU ARE UNDER ARREST.

GET THOSE FORECLAWS WHERE WE CAN SEE 'EM.
DAMN IT--

NO--
DAD. DAD! IT'S OKAY.
SHE CAN HANDLE IT.
PUT 'EM BEHIND YOUR HEAD.
STEP BACK FROM THE JADE STAIRCASE.

HANDLE IT? NO, SHE CAN'T!
THEY'RE GOING TO MAZE HER AND TAKE HER TO JAIL!
I KNOW, VOGO.
DAD, NO--TORGAX SAID YOU ALWAYS CALL THESE FIGHTS "FIRST REELERS". THEY'RE TO SHOW WHAT YOU CAN DO.

NO.
THIS ISN'T A FIRST REEL.
IT'S A THIRD.
THEY'RE GOING TO DEFEAT HER, AND SHE'S GOING TO EXPLODE.

NO.
NO.

DON'T YOU

TOUCH HER

WHAT

KRAK

SKK
DISPATCH
DISPATCH, ARE YOU THERE

DISPATCH, THIS IS **JEONG**
OFFICER **DOWN**
I NEED **BACKUP**

REPEAT--
I NEED BACKUP NOW

Officer JEONG, what is your POSITION?
We'll move the TEAM G.R.E.A.T. SATELLITE into position and TARGET the SUSPECTS with--
NEGATIVE, NEGATIVE!!

WE'RE IN DOWNTOWN ANCHORAGE! YOU'LL VAPORIZE THE WHOLE CITY IF--
HUNGH

SHOOSH
DOOM
Officer JEONG, BACKUP is on its WAY.

Where is your PARTNER? What is her STATUS?
DAMN IT, DISPATCH, THEY HIT HER!
KRAK
I DON'T KNOW WHERE SHE IS--

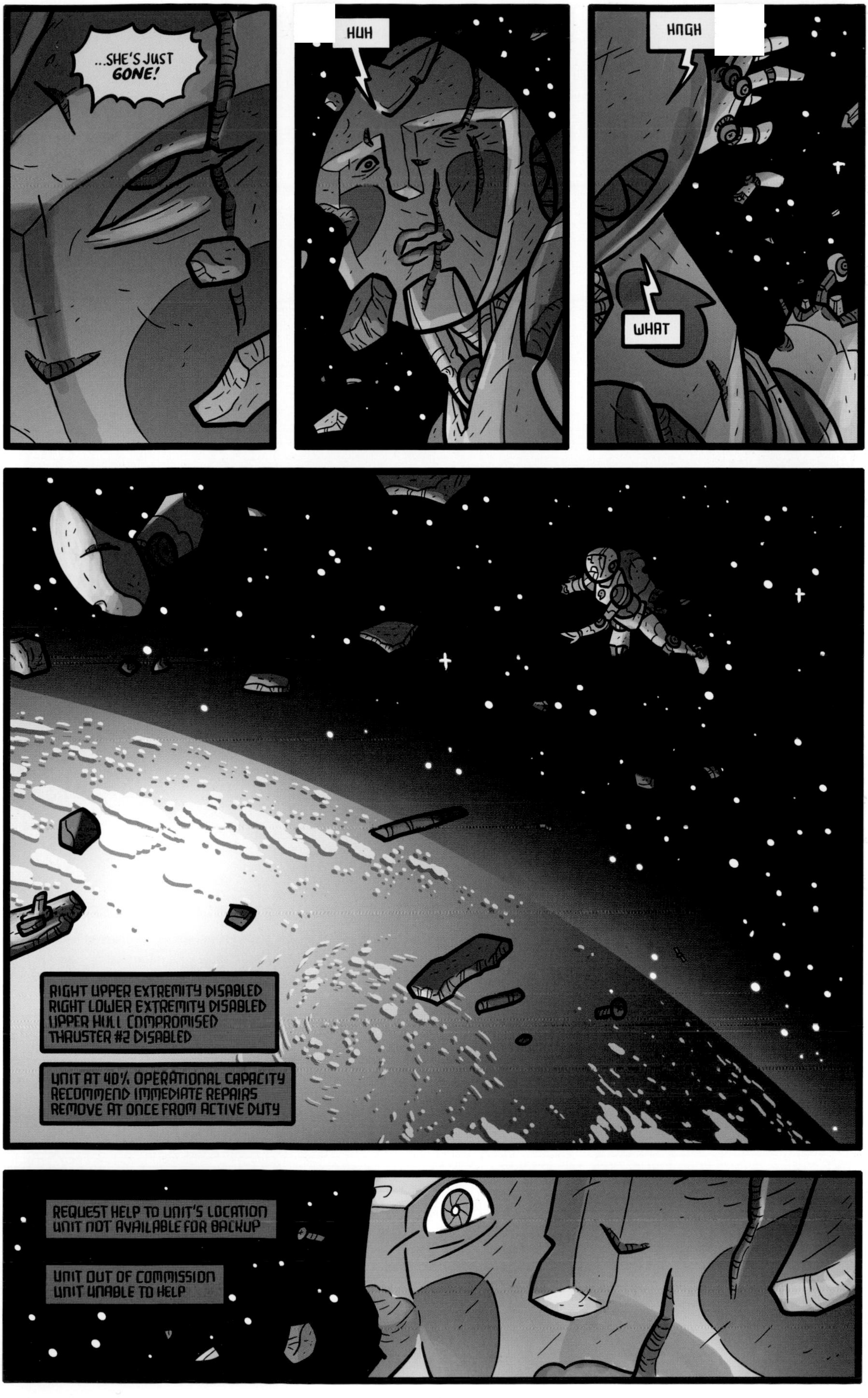

RIGHT UPPER EXTREMITY DISABLED
RIGHT LOWER EXTREMITY DISABLED
UPPER HULL COMPROMISED
THRUSTER #2 DISABLED

UNIT AT 40% OPERATIONAL CAPACITY
RECOMMEND IMMEDIATE REPAIRS
REMOVE AT ONCE FROM ACTIVE DUTY

Stay CALM. We've got a whole BATTALION on the way.
They're fifteen minutes OUT. Hang IN there.

FIFTEEN MISKKSK
GOD DAMN IT, I'M NOT GOING TO MAKESKKS FIVE MINUTXSSKS
THESE TWO ARE GOING TO SSKSSKS KILL SKKSS

WSSKSK
KSSKSSKS
NO

NO
JEONG--

NO--

NO.

YOU HANG IN THERE, JIN-WOOK.
YOU GOD DAMN HANG IN THERE.

I'M YOUR GOD DAMN PARTNER.

AND I'VE GOT YOUR GOD DAMN **BACK.**

AA
SKRKK

HUH

RUN!!
Jin-Wook, RUN!!
Come with ME!

HUH
CHOP

NO!
NO, my son. Listen to ME.
HUSBAND--
NO.
This is ALL as DEAR LEADER has PLANNED.

SLAM

He KNOWS what his LAB has CREATED, my son.
It is up to US to find the LESSON in
FOOOSH
DAD!!

HUH
KRAK

D-DAD!!
RUN, Jin-Wook! RUN!!
RUUN!!

KRUP
HAHH

UFF!
MOTHER!!

SPOKK

COME ON Mother, get UP!
NO, Jin-Wook. You have to RUN!
RUN and FIND someone to keep you SAFE.

AA
OMP

RUN, JIN-WOOK!!
MOTHER!!

WHAM

STOMP

SSKREEE

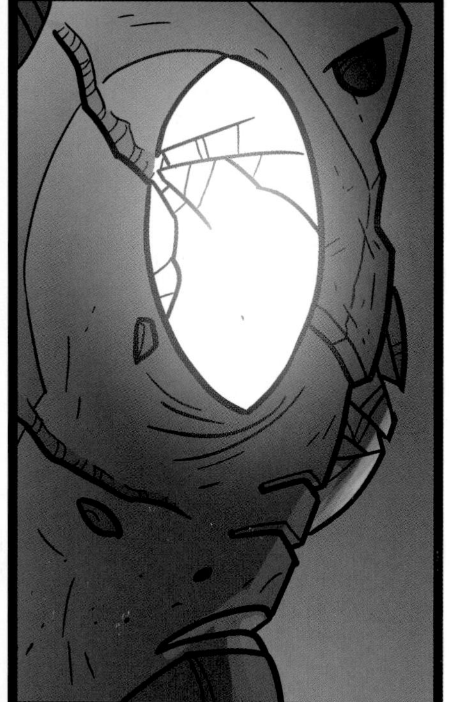

KRAK

HUH
HUH
HUHH
HUFF
OKAY.

YOU OBSERVE YOUR TARGETS. YOU COVER YOUR TRACKS.
YOU COMMIT NO ERRORS.

AND THAT IS HOW YOU SURVIVE.
THAT IS THE ONLY WAY YOU SURVIVE.

SO WE EAT HIM, SO HIS INTERNAL SOULSPARK DOESN'T MARK US OR TRACK US. AND THEN IT'S DONE.
AND THEN WE DON'T HAVE TO LEAVE.

WE CAN STAY HERE, IN OUR PLACE.

TORGAX...

PLEASE, HONEY, IT DOESN'T HAVE TO BE LIKE THIS.
YOU'VE GOTTEN FOOD. YOU'VE TAKEN CARE OF YOUR BROTHER.

BUT I'M BACK NOW.
ME.
DAD.

I'M GOING TO FIX EVERYTHING, HONEY.

I'M GOING TO MAKE EVERYTHING ALL R--

NO

GET DOW

HNNF
KOFF

C-C'MON HONEY, WE GOT TO **GO**--
HNFF **GO?**
LIKE **HELL** WE WILL.
WE HAVE TO TAKE THIS COP AND **EAT** HIM BEFORE THEY--

HEY.

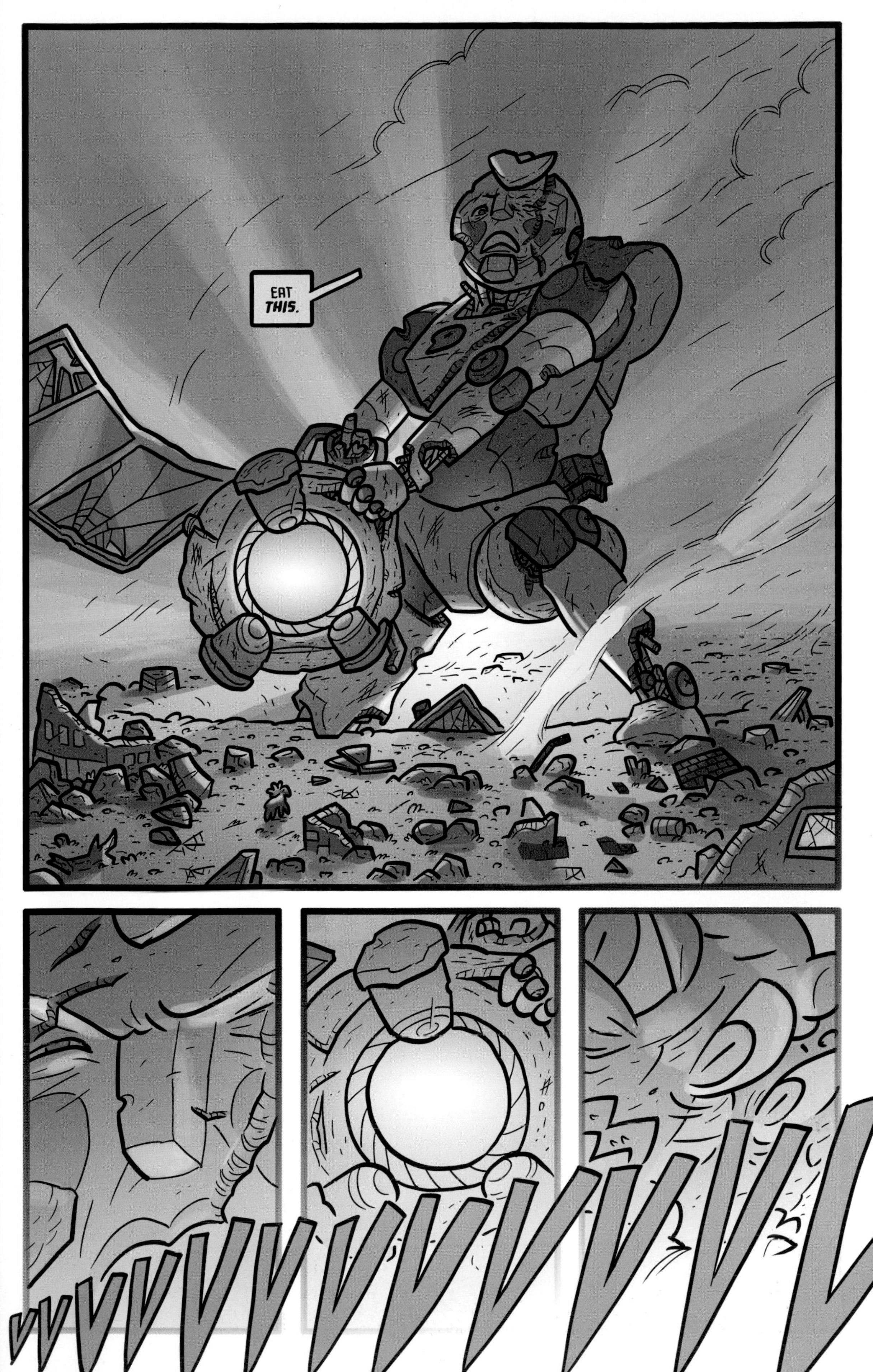
EAT THIS.
VVVVVVVVVVVVVVVVVV

OSS 999 POLICE LINE 999 DO NOT CROSS 999 POLICE LINE 999 DO N
OSS 999
POLICE LINE 999 DO NOT CROSS 999 POLI
LICE LINE 999 DO NOT CROSS 999 POLI

HUH
Gotta get--
I'm gonna--
I'm gonna get squished
I'm gonna get **SQUISHED**
HEY
HEY PARTNER.

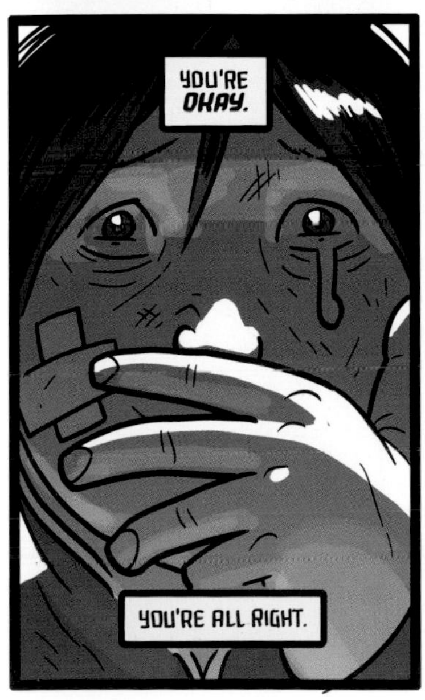

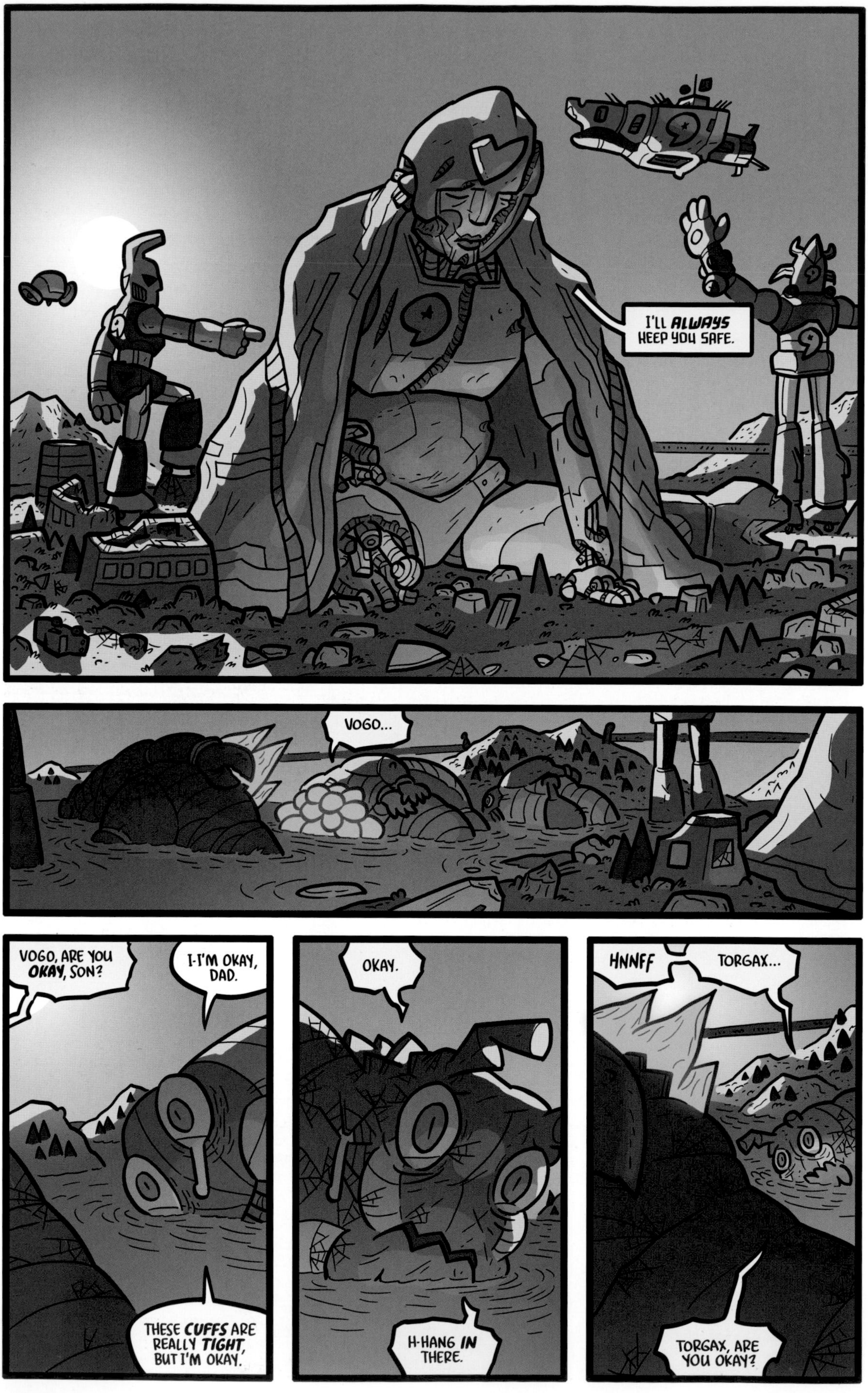

I'LL **ALWAYS** KEEP YOU SAFE.

...TORGAX?

H-HONEY?
I-I JUST WANTED TO SAY...
WH-WHAT YOU **DID** SINCE I WAS **GONE**...

PROTECTING YOUR **BROTHER**...
S-STAYING **HIDDEN**...
FINDING **FOOD**...
PROTECTING OUR **HOME**...
HONEY, **THAT**...
THAT'S **HUGE**.

YOU DID EXACTLY WHAT YOU **SHOULD**. EXACTLY WHAT WAS **NEEDED**.
YOU SAW WHAT LIFE **REQUIRED** OF YOU, AND YOU **DID** IT.

P-**PART** OF ME WANTS TO FEEL LIKE YOU'RE STILL JUST A **LARVA**. LIKE I CAN STILL HOLD YOU IN MY **APPENDAGES**.
BUT YOU'RE **GROWN**. YOU'RE A SMART, STRONG YOUNG **WOMAN**.
AND YOU'VE DONE MORE THAN MONS WHO HAVE BEEN AROUND FOR **MILLIONS** OF YEARS.

END OF SEASON TWO

WANTED
NO
NOW HIRING
Humans only
WE SERVE KAIJU
Takeout only

YOU THINK LIFE OUT IN THE WORLD IS TOUGH, MEGAFAUNA?

BACK ON THE "BIG ISLAND"
IT'S STEP UP OR BE STEPPED ON.

The Creature from Devil's Creek isn't cut out for prison; that much is clear. But when some information comes his way about his tormentors, he finds that he has one last tiny hoof-hold toward getting out from under the Cryptid's control.

Now an enigmatic and rarely-seen crime lord, Whoofy, the Idiot Son of Apewhale, is tormented in private by the terrifying power behind the throne, Li'l Boy. When he realizes he's being used to start a war with another gang, can Whoofy team up with his childhood bully to stop it?

And the morally-compromised Dr. Zhang has broken every rule in the book to sweeten prison life for her paramour, the vicious inmate Zonn. But what has he done for her lately? As Zonn's enemies start looking to settle old scores, Zhang finds out just how many lines she is willing to cross.

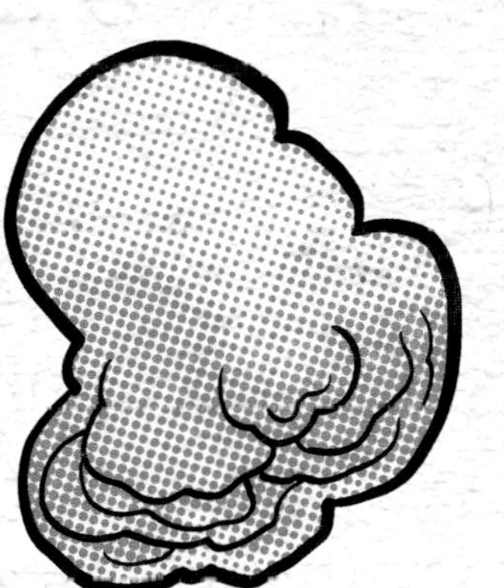

The return of old friends! A new gang in power on the moon! An old mon finds peace after all these years! Vicious murders in the human world!

And... ***our Dark Lord Satan?***

TO BE CONTINUED IN KAIJUMAX: SEASON THREE

CRYPTO-

By Zander Cannon

SATIRE

DESPITE APPEARANCES, I NEVER SET OUT TO MAKE A SOCIAL SATIRE WITH *KAIJUMAX*.

What I initially intended to do was give some giant monsters a little bit of personality and see how they interacted on a Monster Island equivalent. But in the process of giving the book a central hook–the prison drama–I found that, along with providing me with myriad jokes and funny juxtapositions, it also chucked me headlong into a decidedly gray moral universe. The classic prison–and, in this season, crime drama–scenes that anchor this book give a larger sense of futility, amorality, and despair, and the basic premise of kaiju being Earth's unwanted leads *KAIJUMAX* to mirror certain current events and unjust realities of the world we live in.

People have written volumes about how science fiction and fantasy can be used to tackle social issues in a very pure way. With a little metaphorical trickery, it allows us to stack the deck a bit and deliver a premise and a story arc without every real-world counterargument coming into it. But there are pitfalls here. If you hew too close to a specific, real concept, (e.g. kaiju type X equals racial group Y), you enter a dangerous area. At the very least people will get bored, once they've "figured it out", so to speak, but it also puts you at risk of allowing your science fiction plot to maneuver you into saying something that advances the story but is inaccurate or ugly about a real-world group of people.

By design, *KAIJUMAX* maintains only an inch-thin logical structure to its world precisely for this reason. I want to play out each scene as an homage to both monster and prison movies, as well as a take on a philosophical or social concept, and show how these pressures affect individuals. It's not necessarily important to me to explore the precise mechanics of how 50 meter tall robots might work. But I do contend that the inch of worldbuilding is very important; saying that one situation is "kinda like" another is heck of a lot more reasonable, more respectful, and more interesting writing than saying a real type of person is represented by a city stomping monster. We all have enough problems without being equated to some sort of disaster metaphor.

I consider myself a thoughtful person and I'm a bit sentimental (being a dad will do that to you). I am acutely aware of the dangers of commenting on such things as race and class and injustice in a forum as preposterous and humor-based as this comic book. Comics that have the same type of X-meets-Y premise as *KAIJUMAX* can tend to lean on some pretty old and moldy stereotypes for a laugh or for an antagonist, but it's my opinion that for several reasons – basic human decency foremost among them – we ought to go for more empathy rather than less. If we can look at a religious zealot robot, or a blue-collar ex-con kaiju, or an anxiety-ridden transforming superhero, or a Elder God who's fallen through the cracks and see a little bit of ourselves there, well, maybe there's hope for this old world after all.

SINCE 1993, ***ZANDER CANNON*** HAS WRITTEN AND DRAWN COMICS ABOUT GODS, ROBOTS, ASTRONAUTS, POLICE OFFICERS, PALEONTOLOGISTS, ALIENS, FENG SHUI MASTERS, SUPERHEROES, AND MONSTERS.

HE LIVES IN MINNESOTA WITH HIS STRONG WIFE JULIE AND ABOVE-AVERAGE SON JIN.

KAIJUMAX.COM
@ZANDER_CANNON